# LIVING
# ORIGINALLY

### TEN SPIRITUAL PRACTICES TO
### TRANSFORM YOUR LIFE

Robert Brumet

## ALSO BY THE AUTHOR

*Birthing a Greater Reality*

*The Quest for Wholeness*

*Finding Yourself in Transition*

# LIVING
# ORIGINALLY

## TEN SPIRITUAL PRACTICES TO
### TRANSFORM YOUR LIFE

Robert Brumet

unity® Books

Unity Village, Missouri

# Living Originally

A Unity Books Paperback Original

Unity Books are available at special discounts for bulk purchases for study groups, book clubs, sales promotions, book signings, or fundraising. To place an order, call the Unity Customer Care Department at 1-866-236-3571 or email *wholesaleaccts @unityonline.org*.

Bible quotations are from the Revised Standard Version unless otherwise noted.

Cover design: Terry Newell
Interior design: The Covington Group, Kansas City, Missouri

Library of Congress Control Number: 2012955846

ISBN: 978-0-87159-360-3

Canada BN 13252 0933 RT

# ACKNOWLEDGEMENTS

As I was writing this manuscript, I became aware of the many authors, teachers, and teachings that lie behind almost every sentence in this book. Though far too numerous to mention individually, I want to make a general acknowledgement of all the teachers and writers who have been impactful on my spiritual journey and who are, in some way, embodied in the words printed in this book. I feel an immense amount of gratitude for each of them.

I want to acknowledge many friends and family members who have provided me with support and encouragement in the yearlong journey of writing this book. In particular, I want to thank Michael Maday, Shellie Bassett, Kelly Ludden, and Stephanie Stokes Oliver for their editorial feedback and administrative assistance.

I also want to acknowledge my colleagues and students at Unity School of Christianity and Unity Institute for their support and encouragement in this writing project. Finally, I express my gratitude for the Unity movement itself, and for all of the dedicated and talented people I have had the honor of meeting throughout the past 35 years.

# Bonus Meditations

Author Robert Brumet has written and recorded audio meditations for the 10 spiritual practices in *Living Originally*. Listen or download at *unitybooks.org/living*.

# CONTENTS

# INTRODUCTION

The term *living originally* seems to make reference to a particular lifestyle that is different from that of most people. To most of us, the word *original* means "unique." Let me introduce a different perspective to the meaning of *living originally*. I will begin by quoting author Cynthia Bourgeault, "In the actual meaning of the word, however, being original doesn't mean trying to be different. It means *being connected to the origin*. You can't be original by trying to be original. You become original by staying true to what your heart sees."[1]

To live originally is to live consciously from the ever-present origin[2] of life; it is to live from the very source of all that is. This ever-present origin is centered within each of us. We all live from that origin, but the vast majority of us are not conscious of this. Most of us live unconsciously because we have become identified with a false self; we live with a mistaken identity. This false self is the product of our conditioning; it is a manufactured sense of self. It is unoriginal.

As humans we have relatively few inborn survival instincts. Unlike most animals, our survival skills arise not so much from instinct as from culture. These survival skills are conveyed primarily by family when we are very young and by our teachers and peers as we get older. This conditioning, this enculturation, is necessary for us to survive and to relate to others in our culture.

This conditioned self is like a mask. It is a persona: a personality. Though it is necessary for survival, when we become exclusively identified with it, we lose awareness of our true origin. The problem is not with the personality per se—the problem is identification with it as our one and only self. As such, we no longer live originally; we live by the dictates of our conditioning.

It's considered pathological in our culture to not have a functional personality. We consider it normal to believe that the personality is who we really are. But this is actually just a higher form of pathology. When we are alienated from our origin, we do not live originally or authentically. We live according to our conditioning and its responses to our environment; we live mechanically rather than authentically.

To live originally is to live from the center of one's being. Living originally means living from the inside out, from center to circumference. In our conditioned existence, identified with personality, we live from the outside in; we live from circumference to center. As the personality, who we are and what we believe, think, and feel is largely determined by the world around us. As a product of our environment, we are defined by it and are subject to its vicissitudes.

To live originally is to live authentically, to not be defined by culture or environment, to be truly oneself. We do not want to ignore culture. We live in it; but we need not be defined by it. Living originally, we are *in* the world but we are not *of* the world.

Identified with a false self, we live egocentrically, defined by our needs and by the strategies used to fulfill those needs. Living originally does not deny the existence of our needs, but it knows we are not defined by them. Our needs do not control us. They do not dictate our purpose for being alive.

Shifting from an egocentric life to living originally requires more than a change in lifestyle and more than a new worldview. It requires a complete shift in one's consciousness. It is even more than a conversion—it is a transformation.

Transformation is the process whereby we shift our identity from the personality to the authentic self. As the identity shifts, so does our experience of reality itself. Transformation propels us into the experience of living originally in every facet of our life. We will now turn our attention to this process of transformation.

# 1. TRANSFORMATION

The small band of terrorists moved slowly toward Damascus. They were on a search-and-destroy mission. Having killed before, they would readily do it again … What happened next would change the course of human history.

Suddenly, a blinding flash of light appeared. Their leader, one Saul of Tarsus, heard a voice which said, "Saul, Saul, why do you persecute me?" (Acts 9:4) These words would change his life forever. This man would eventually become the greatest proponent of the very religion he sought to destroy. Historically, Saul is best known by his Roman name "Paul." Once a persecutor of Christians, he went on to become one of Christianity's greatest advocates.

It is one of history's greatest ironies that one who fanatically opposed the new movement would go on to teach, preach, and promote this same movement with tireless zeal and dauntless courage. Paul's efforts would deeply impact the lives of more than a billion people throughout the next 2,000 years.

Most of us are not as fanatical as Paul was, and perhaps have no desire to be as Paul became, yet few of us cannot but be impressed by the power of the transformation that took place in his life. Not all transformations are as dramatic or historically impactful as was Paul's. Most transformative experiences are more gradual and less visible to an outsider. Yet the power of this experience cannot be overstated. A life transformed is radically different from one's former life: One's sense of self has radically shifted; one's values and priorities have been radically redefined. A life transformed is lived with radically new meaning and sense of purpose. It is a life that is lived originally.

In this chapter, we will explore the topic of transformation. We look at what it is, what it means, and if it is even possible to us ordinary individuals. We begin with a dictionary definition that says to transform is "to change the condition, nature, or function of something ..." I use *transformation* to mean all of this, and to mean it in a very deep and personal sense. I use this term to mean *self-transformation*: The transformation of the self.

Transformation is a radical shift in one's identity and one's worldview. It is a shift in consciousness to a much larger and deeper view of oneself and of the universe. It is a quantum leap into a new way of being. It is awakening to an entirely new reality, to an authentic and an original life. It always contains the experience of greater freedom, power, and love than hitherto could be imagined.

Transformation is an internal and invisible process, but it ultimately impacts the visible and external aspects of our life: Our health, our relationships, and our work. Every facet of our being in the world is deeply impacted by this internal shift.

No two transformative experiences are exactly alike, yet there is a common denominator in every such experience: One's identity is no longer fixated on a separated isolated self that is preoccupied with its own needs and interests. We experience an increased sense of freedom, a new sense of purpose, and a sense of fearlessness. Our morals and values become internalized and are less defined by others or by the culture. And yet, we become exquisitely sensitive to the well-being of others. This sensitivity emanates from a genuine compassion rather than from an ego-centered need to be liked, to be good, or to belong.

Transformation means discovering a whole new dimension of reality. Imagine you live in a two-dimensional world. Your entire sense of reality is confined to east and west, north and south—you know nothing else. Then suddenly, you hear a voice from a three-dimensional being who tells you to "move upward." This makes no sense to you! You say, "Upward? Speak to me in English! Do you mean east, west, north, or south? There is nowhere else to go! *Upward* has no meaning to me!" The third dimension would be beyond the scope of our understanding.

The experience of transformation cannot be fully understood by anyone unaware of this dimension. Throughout history, sages and mystics have been met with scorn and skepticism. It is like trying to explain the color red to a man that was blind since birth. If there is no internal recognition of a word, all descriptions are for naught.

We cannot adequately describe transformation in words, but we can describe a path that can lead to transformation. We cannot adequately describe the color red to the blind man, but perhaps we can help him gain his sight so that he may experience the color red directly and personally. This is the purpose of all transformational spiritual practice.

## Transformation vs. Translation

We usually find transformational teachings within the genre of spiritual or religious teachings. Transformation is always spiritual, but it is not necessarily religious in nature. Religious language and imagery is often used to describe many transformational experiences, but certainly not all of them. Transformation can also be described in psychological or in scientific language, but it is most often described by parable, poetry, art, or music.

All transformation is inherently spiritual in nature, but not all teachings identified as "spiritual" are necessarily transformational. There are many spiritual teachings that do not point to a new reality or a new identity. Their aim is for the individual to function better within the existing self/reality system. These may be called *translational* teachings; they seek to improve our life rather than to transform it.[3] Rather than point to another dimension, they point to new possibilities within the known dimensions of life.

Translational teachings have been helpful to many people. They can help to make life work better. They can help us to develop better relationships, better health, and more prosperity. And perhaps more important, they often provide a source of comfort and consolation amid the difficulties of life.

But for some, self-improvement and consolation is not enough. More than comfort and consolation, they want complete freedom, unconditional peace of mind, and the experience of a deeper reality. For these individuals, our everyday reality is seen as a dream state, and they seek to awaken from the dream, rather than simply improve upon it.

Translational teachings strive to make the ego more comfortable and more in control. But transformational teachings challenge the arrogance and the delusions of the ego; they turn its world upside down and inside out. One well-known Buddhist teacher would often say, "From the perspective of the ego, this journey is just one insult after another!" Such is the nature of transformation!

Yet many of us would rather be insulted by reality than comforted by our delusions. Having experienced the egocentric life and found it to be wanting, we prefer truth to comfort, reality to consolation. Finding the former icons of comfort and security to be very hollow, we feel guided by an internal longing for the unnamed and the unknown. It would seem something in us has shifted. We don't know why, how, or where it will lead us—but we are willing to follow it.

That which calls us may be called the ever-present origin, the ground of being, true nature, higher power, Christ within, or a variety of other names. Whatever we call it, it is infinitely more real than the egoic self. Although it makes no promises, we can sense that it beckons us to a new life; we sense a new reality latent at our core.

This beckoning is the call to transformation. It can become very strong and persistent; yet we always have a choice in how we respond. We are never coerced; but once we discover this pearl, we are never the same. In the Gospel of Matthew, we find the parable of a merchant searching for pearls. The merchant finds one pearl of great value. So great is its value that he sells everything he owns in order to purchase it.[4]

To "sell all that we own" is not easy, but when we consider the deeper meaning of this parable, we see that it ultimately means to let go of all our attachments—both external and (more important) internal. We must eventually release all we believe we are. Shedding our material possessions is of little value if we remain attached to our present sense of selfhood.*

This call to a new life is the call to a new form of humanity—one that is no longer motivated by self-centered interests. Yet it is not simply altruism or "doing good" toward which the new life is calling. Rather, it is to go beyond our self as we are now, because we intuitively know we truly *are more* than we have previously experienced ourselves to be.

We are being called to go beyond our self not because this self is bad, but because we are being called to *grow up*. Our present egoic level of development was never meant to be the final stage of our evolution. This present stage is a bit like adolescence—necessary, but not a good place to stay! If our current level of development was meant to be the end of our evolution, then the human race may have been doomed from the start, because we cannot sustain 7 billion self-centered egos on this

---

*My experience is that when we let go of the internal attachments, we may not always need to let go of the externals, but ironically, *we may need to lose the external attachment in order to let go of an internal attachment*. Eventually, we learn we will have all we need (externally) if there is no (internal) attachment to any of it. "But **seek first his kingdom** and his righteousness, and all these things shall be yours as well" (Mt. 6:33).

planet! Like a plague of locusts, we are destroying the very resources that give us our life.

Translational teachings are aimed at finding a new and more functional image of one's self, whereas transformation is about transcending all self-images. Transformation is the freedom to function beyond the confines of any fixed identity.

We typically carry an image of what we wish to become. But in the transformational journey, it's important not to be attached to any image of what we seek to become. *What we are looking for is that which is looking.* What we become is what we have always truly been—yet have never known.

Transformation may be likened to seeing our Earth from outer space. In a way, we are seeing Earth for the very first time. We see it every day, but from a very limited point of view. We stand upon it, but we do not really see it because our perspective is too small. From outer space we see the immensity and the beauty of that which we have always stood upon but have seldom recognized. With transformation we see the power and the beauty of that which we have always been living in and upon: the ever-present origin; the ground of all that exists.

### The Role of Personal Will

A question inherent in this discussion is whether or not transformation is something one can make happen. Can we will it to occur? The answer seems to be "no"; however, having the desire for transformation is an essential ingredient. Desire may be necessary, but it alone is not sufficient.

Egocentric desires typically arise from a sense of deficiency and from resistance to our present experience: "I desire food because I am hungry; I desire a friend because I am lonely." It may attempt to approach transformational practice with this very same attitude. The ego can believe it wants transformation because it secretly believes that "when I am transformed I will have no more problems, no more pain, and will always feel safe and comfortable." Transformation becomes one more strategy the ego employs to feel safe, comfortable, and in control.

One of the essential elements in spiritual practice is "right intention."[5] It's very important to ask, "Does this intention arise from the authentic self or from the ego?" Discernment of desire is an essential element of any transformational spiritual practice. Desire for transformation is necessary to provide the motivation to engage spiritual practice; however, it is also necessary to surrender our attachment to the object or the image of our desires.

Surrender is also an essential part of transformational practice. Surrender is not to anything or anyone outside of our self; it is surrendering to our own authentic self. Most of our resistance to surrender is unconscious. When we consciously choose to surrender, we will begin to see subconscious resistance arise, and we soon see the myriad ways in which we deceive ourselves. We begin to see that resistance and deception is the foundation of the ego itself!

The ego can sometimes act like it has completely surrendered—but then it wants to be at its own funeral, delivering its own eulogy! We may find our self secretly striking a bargain: "Yes, I will surrender completely because that's the best way to get what I want." True surrender is not instrumental; it is not for the purpose of gaining anything that we don't already have.

Honesty is an essential ingredient on this path. It can sometimes take brutal honesty to look at the subtle ways that we deceive ourselves—and perhaps deceive others as well. True surrender cannot occur without complete honesty, and complete honesty cannot occur without genuine right intention.

Personal will plays a paradoxical role in transformation. We cannot be transformed simply through willpower, yet we must be willing to allow transformation to occur. Paradoxically, we must have the "will to surrender our will," but we cannot force surrender to occur, any more than we can force transformation to occur.

And yet we should not sit idly and just wait for transformation to happen. Like the farmer, we cannot force the seeds to grow, but we can plant the seeds and cultivate the proper conditions for the ripening and the flowering of transformation. Spiritual practice is the way we "cultivate the soil" for transformation to blossom.

### Paul's Teachings on Transformation

Let us now return to the apostle Paul for some clues on how we may cultivate our transformation.[6] In his letter to the Galatians, Paul writes, "I have been crucified with Christ; it is no longer I who live, but Christ who lives in me" (Gal. 2:20). Transformation involves a crucifixion of one's former egocentric self and a rebirth to the Christ within—our true nature. Obviously, Paul was not referring to a physical crucifixion. He was instead referring to a symbolic death, the death of an egocentric way of life. The self-centered, self-serving personality is crucified, or crossed out, and a new self emerges.

Jesus referred to this principle when he said to his disciples, "He who finds his life will lose it, and he who loses his life for my sake will find it" (Mt. 10:39). This enigmatic statement refers to a form of giving up or losing one's personal life and then finding and living from the life of the Christ within, which is the universal life—the life abundant. Transformation involves the sacrifice of the particular for the universal, the limited for the unlimited, the temporal for the eternal.

In Paul's letter to the Romans, he writes, "Do not be conformed to this world but be transformed by the renewal of your mind, that you may prove what is the will of God, what is good and acceptable and perfect" (12:2). He echoed a similar teaching in his letter to the Ephesians: "Put off your old nature which belongs to your former manner of life and is corrupt through deceitful lusts, and be renewed in the spirit of your minds, and put on the new nature, created after the likeness of God in true righteousness and holiness" (4:22-24). In both teachings, Paul refers to the "renewing of the mind" and herein lies another key to transformation.

To renew the mind, Paul tells us, is to conform no longer to the appearances and the beliefs of this world. He tells us that we must release the old nature, for it is "corrupt through deceitful lusts." This is far more than a teaching of morality. It is a teaching of radical transformation—a complete shift in one's level of being. The old nature is corrupt in that it does not know the truth; it conforms to the world of appearance and illusion. The old nature is corrupt through "deceitful lusts." This refers to the two characteristics of an ego-centered life: greed and delusion. To put off this old nature and to no longer conform to this world is to release our self-centered greediness and to give up our faith in the reality of appearances.

The old nature is self-centered, greedy, and lustful, because it is based on the premise that we are separated from the rest of life and from one another. This belief in separateness leads to a life based on "not-enough-ness." Separation creates the fear of not doing enough, of not having enough, of not being enough. Greed arises from this fear. Yet the truth is that if we live in the experience of separation, we can *never* do enough, have enough, or be enough. Humans have exploited the earth and each other for many thousands of years in a vain attempt to fill the emptiness created from their belief in separation.

The old nature is delusional. It believes that it sees reality, yet what it sees is the product of its own imaginings. In the unawakened state, we don't see things as they are; we see things as we are. We project onto the world around us the images that lurk within the shadows of our own minds. Unmindful of the self-created demons within us, we project them onto our environment. Then, like Don Quixote, we spend our time "doing battle with windmills," convinced of our own rightness and righteousness.

Yet it is important that we not judge the ego as evil or bad, for it is not. A caterpillar is not bad simply because it does not have the freedom or the beauty of the butterfly. A child is not bad just because he or she does not have the knowledge or the strength of an adult. One of the steps in the transformative process is to appreciate the life we've lived until now and know that every experience was necessary to bring us to this point of readiness for transformation.

"Do not be conformed" means much more than superficially embracing nonconformity or simply rebelling against tradition or authority. Such a rebellion may be an attempt to become free of the shackles of limitation, but mere rebellion simply substitutes one form of bondage for another. To become a true nonconformist is to step outside the delusions that keep us in bondage. A true nonconformist demonstrates how to live originally.

Ralph Waldo Emerson wrote:

> It is easy in the world to live after the world's opinion; it is easy in solitude to live after our own; but the great man is he who in the midst of the crowd keeps with perfect sweetness the independence of solitude.[7]

This is the nature of true nonconformity. To not be conformed to the world is to have the courage to trust our own intuition, even if it conforms not to the teachings of this world's authorities. It means to put faith in our inner knowing of truth more than to succumb to the voice of authority and, perhaps, even to the voice of reason.

Reason can certainly serve a useful purpose, yet it can easily be duped if it is divorced from the heart. For many years "reasonable" men have argued for the necessity of slavery, for the oppression of women and children, and for the exploitation of our environment.

Emerson also wrote:

A man should learn to detect and watch that gleam of light which flashes across his mind from within, more than the lustre of the firmament of bards and sages. Yet he dismisses without notice his thought, because it is his. In every work of genius we recognize our own rejected thoughts; they come back to us with a certain alienated majesty.[8]

True genius is simply having the courage and the faith to live outside the mind that is conforming to this world and to live within the transformed mind that is "created after the likeness of God in true righteousness and holiness."

To appreciate the life we have lived and to see it as the foundation for the next stage of our journey is to take a major step in preparing for transformation. To have the courage and the faith to trust in and live from the intuitive voice within is to take another step. This is the beginning of "the renewing of the mind."

## Adversity and Transformation

Sometimes adversity prepares us for transformation. To be sure, adversity in and of itself does not necessarily transform us. But when we meet adversity with a clear mind and an open heart, the adverse experience can serve as a catalyst for opening us to deeper levels of self than might normally be possible. When we face adversity with awareness, acceptance, and appreciation, we release layers of the old nature, the old mind, and facilitate the awakening of the new Mind—the Christ within.

The death of the old self, always a prelude to transformation, is often catalyzed by some adverse experience in our lives. To the old self, the ego, something is drastically wrong! We may want to do anything but face the challenge that lies before us. When we feel stretched beyond our limits or feel defeated beyond any human capacity to recover, we are ripe for transformation. An old proverb says that man's extremity is God's opportunity. When the human ego feels crushed and crucified, the opportunity for transformation is at hand. Our work at this point is to surrender. In the garden of Gethsemane, just before his crucifixion, Jesus said, "My Father ... thy will be done" (Mt. 26:42). This is what we are to do.

This surrender, however, is not done with an attitude of resignation or despair, but with an attitude of self-awareness, acceptance, and appreciation. We cannot be forced into transformation. We must go willingly—indeed, joyfully. To see adversity as a gift is to ready oneself for transformation. This is not easy to do. When we are caught up in appearances and in strong emotions, appreciating the big picture is difficult. When we are caught up in great pain or fear, it seems that nothing matters but getting out of it! Yet if we have the courage to keep our hearts and minds open to the possibility of the greater freedom that is incipient within the challenge itself, we are opening the door to a greater reality.

Rachel Naomi Remen, M.D., tells of a woman who had lived most of her life in bitterness and isolation from others. While having a bone marrow transplant, she found herself filled with anger, envy, and resentment. She was overwhelmed by self-pity and experienced a sense of isolation so profound that it was beyond words. She had never before let herself feel at this depth.

As she surrendered into this experience and allowed it to burn away the beliefs that separated her from others, it left her with an unshakable sense of belonging and connection to all life. She had found her way to the simplicity of an open heart and from this came an enduring inner change and a natural open-hearted kindness toward others.[9]

Awareness, acceptance, trust, and appreciation are all attitudes that ripen us for transformation. This is especially so when we can continue to maintain these qualities of mind and heart during times of adversity. To be "crucified with a smile on our face" is extremely powerful and, in a certain sense, is necessary for transformation.

This is *not* to advocate martyrdom, victimhood, or self-punishment; that does not prepare us for transformation. However, when life brings adversity unbidden, it is very important that we not react with resistance and judgment. "Not my will, but thine, be done" (Lk. 22:42) is a very powerful prayer and one that prepares the way for the "renewing of the mind."

Transformation is paradoxical. It is indeed "passing beyond" the self as it is, and yet in another sense, it is simply becoming more of what one already is. We can see it as a process of transcendence—moving beyond; yet we can also see it as a deepening—moving into the very nature of our own being and living fully and creatively from that deeper nature. In either way of seeing it, transformation is a movement, a quantum leap, into a new way of life, a new way of being.

Having discussed the nature of transformation, we now turn our attention to the process of cultivating the soil for transformation via spiritual practice.

# 2. ENGAGING THE PRACTICES

The seeds of transformation lie within each of us awaiting activation. We cannot control when or how these seeds will come into fruition, but we can develop the conditions that nurture and support the seeds of transformation. We do this through spiritual practice.

## The Nature of Spiritual Practice

Transformational spiritual practice has both active and passive elements. The passive element is to deliberately refrain from activities that substantiate and reinforce the egocentric identity. We practice by not doing that which is familiar and habitual. For example, we may sit quietly and do nothing but pay attention to our breath. Sooner or later we will notice uncomfortable physical sensations, distracting thoughts and desires arising, and many stories beckoning us to indulge in them. The practice then is to simply notice this without reacting and then return to the breath. We do not indulge the ego's demand for our attention. This is the practice of "not doing."

The active element of transformational practice is to intentionally engage in activities that disrupt the habituated patterns of the egocentric identity. For example, we may engage in a practice of generosity that will bring to the surface the egocentric tendencies toward selfishness or possessiveness; it may uncover our fear of lack or limitation. We then look directly at these beliefs and their resultant emotions. We are then able to make the conscious choice to believe them no more as we continue our practice of generosity.

Ego-identification feeds upon attention for its survival. As we engage a spiritual practice that refuses to feed this habituated pattern, the egoic tendencies will gradually disappear, but first they will assert themselves with vigor. Rather than act upon or suppress this impulse, as we might habitually do, we allow the impulse to arise, we notice it, and we simply return to our practice. We make a conscious choice to neither reject nor act upon the impulses that arise.

Eventually these impulses will diminish; but not without a great deal of protesting! This is why strong intention and commitment to practice is vital. The ego-identity will demand that we feed it with our attention and our agreement with its beliefs and its stories. Spiritual practice is intentionally interrupting our habituated tendency to do this.

For example, the ego-self may have a strong propensity for planning and always anticipating future events. A spiritual practice such as meditation will persistently call us back to our present moment experience, interrupting the mind's tendency toward futurizing. Returning to the present moment, we may see that this compulsive planning is a smokescreen for some underlying pain that's calling for our attention. The healing of this will occur only by accepting it in the present moment.

With transformational spiritual practice, we are not trying to attain a particular experience or to reach a desired goal. We are not trying to feel a certain way, nor are we trying to solve any personal problems. Our primary intention is to simply engage the chosen practice without any attachment to a specific outcome.

As a result of practice, we may have some euphoric experiences or gain some profound insights, but we see this simply as a by-product of our practice, not the primary goal. Conversely, we may have some unpleasant or difficult experiences along the way. It is very important not to become discouraged. This is where a teacher or a support group can be of help to us.

As we engage these practices, we do not ignore our human responsibilities. We continue to do what needs to be done in accord with our life circumstances. We pay our bills, show up for appointments, and fulfill the commitments we have made. Ethical and responsible behavior is always a foundation for transformational spiritual practice.

We can use our life circumstances as a catalyst for transformation, but our circumstances should not be the primary focus of our practice (unless we are confronted with a life-or-death situation). We do not try to control anything but our attention and our own behavior. As a result of our practice, we may sometimes experience great delight and sometimes experience great discomfort; either way, we simply do the practice without attachment or resistance to our experience.

In spiritual practice, we will not always "do it right" in the conventional sense of that phrase. We create an intention and we do our best to stay with it; but it is inevitable that we will falter along the way. This apparent faltering is *not* a failure and *is* a very important part of the practice. How we respond to this experience is crucial. It is not helpful to berate ourselves or to get frustrated; nor is it helpful to just ignore the fact that we have strayed from our intention.

The skillful approach is to notice you have strayed from the intended path, and to notice this with no judgment whatsoever. Then notice what it was that has pulled you away from your intention: It may be a physical sensation, a sound, a thought, an emotion, or a desire. Notice this without reacting to it and then return to the practice.

In noticing without judgment what has captured your attention, you will begin to see habituated ego patterns and the power they seem to have. Seeing this without judgment, without resistance, and without analysis or interpretation, is the beginning of becoming free from these habituated patterns. Freedom comes from awareness without resistance.

If there is judgment or resistance, or if you do get caught up in the ego's stories, then just notice this as soon as possible, and return to the practice without any more judgment or commentary.

The new Zen student came before the master and bowed. "What sir is the most important thing that I learn?" The master closed his eyes, paused, and replied, "Good judgment." The student bowed again and said, "Thank you, and how do I attain good judgment?" The master again closed his eyes, paused, and replied, "Bad judgment."

We can learn much from our so-called mistakes and shortcomings. This is indeed an essential part of any learning process. Strong intention without self-judgment and without attachment to results is crucial as we engage our spiritual practice.

As we do our various practices, we allow thoughts, feelings, and sensations to arise naturally. We do not cling to or reject any of them. We neither believe nor disbelieve whatever arises. We simply notice it and then return to our practice. If we do get caught up in attachment or resistance, we just notice that and then once again return to the practice. We always return to the intention of our spiritual practice.

This intention is a guide rather than a goal; it is the "compass needle" that guides our progress in the chosen direction. If you were in the wilderness and wanted to travel due north, you would consult your compass and then walk, as best you can, in the direction that the arrow points. At times you will stray from your course, and at times you will encounter an obstacle that prohibits you from proceeding due north; but you will always return the attention to your compass needle and follow the course as best you can, given the terrain you are traversing. You simply continue the journey despite any obstacles in your way or past mistakes that you have made. Like the compass needle, your intention is what guides you. This is how we do our spiritual practice.

Having a spiritual support group can be helpful. We often need support for our practice, as well as help in seeing our own blind spots. Having others who share the practice and provide mutual support can make a big difference in sustaining our practice.

## Engaging the Practices

This book is about spiritual practice. Its purpose is to describe and prescribe certain practices to support transformation. *This book is meant to be read, and then applied, chapter by chapter.* It may be edifying to simply read the book from cover to cover without engaging the practices, but this is like reading the menu in a restaurant without ordering a meal. You could read the menu at every restaurant in town, but this alone will never satisfy your hunger. Enjoy the menu, but more important, enjoy the meal!

Engaging a spiritual practice is similar to learning a new skill. Let's use tennis as an analogy. If you want to learn how to play tennis, you might begin by reading a book or viewing a video. It may work best if you study for a bit and then get out on the court and practice the skills described. These skills are best learned in a progressive fashion. You would start with the basic ground strokes—forehand and backhand—and then you might work on the volley and then the serve. These basic skills must be established before you can master the finer points of the game, such as playing strategies and specialty shots.

Typically, you would choose a particular stroke and then engage in a drill; perhaps hitting only forehands for 10 minutes and then backhands for 10 minutes and then alternating forehand and backhand. When you play a match with your friends, you will attempt to integrate these skills into the actual game.

You might have developed a skillful backhand in a drill, but using it in a game can be much more challenging! But that's how we *really* learn to play tennis. The study and the drills only prepare us for the real game. Yet it is vitally important we take the time to learn and to practice if we really want to improve our game of tennis.

And so it is with spiritual practice. The following pages will describe the basic practices. You may be given a specific exercise or formal practice such as a 20-minute sitting meditation. But the real work is always taking the skill into the "game" of our everyday life. That is where we are really transformed. A Zen proverb says, "If you want a small enlightenment, go to the mountain (where the temple is). If you want a big enlightenment, go to the city (where the people are)."

After reading this chapter, we recommend you read Chapter 3 (Practice 1) and then engage the practice for a fixed period of time before reading Chapter 4 (Practice 2). Reading chapters beyond the current practice can be confusing and may interfere with the skillful application of the practice at hand. These practices generally build one upon another; each practice forms the foundation for the next. This is especially true for the first five practices.

**The Core Practices**

The first five practices are called the *core practices*. The first two are the *self-related* practices. These are the practices of Radical Self-Awareness and Deep Self-Acceptance. These practices address your relationship with each moment-by-moment experience; thus they address your primary relationship with life itself. These two practices form the core of all the other practices. Unless these first two practices are mastered with at least a minimum degree of skill, the other practices cannot be performed effectively.

Practices 1 and 2 are self-related because the focus is on your personal internal experience moment by moment. The practice addresses your relationship to each internal experience of thinking, feeling, sensing, and so on. Practices 1 and 2 are presented as separate practices, but after practicing them for a while, they will seem to be inseparable.

The next three practices (Unlimited Forgiveness, Universal Benevolence, and Compassionate Communication) form the core practices involving your relationship with others. These are called *other-related* practices. The practice of Unlimited Forgiveness also applies to oneself, so it falls into both categories. For the sake of simplicity, we will group it with the other-related practices.

You will find that the focus of Practices 3, 4, and 5 are interrelated, and as your practice continues, these three may also seem to merge into one practice. Eventually the self-related and other-related practices may themselves begin to naturally merge together. In a tennis game, a skilled player does not consciously think, "Now I should hit a forehand volley and then a backhand ground stroke and then an overhead smash." She will simply play the game organically, integrating all of the skills learned in practice.

Likewise, we begin by practicing each skill individually, but eventually we integrate them into our everyday life. The five core practices can become the foundation for how we relate to self and others, and the foundation for how we relate to our life itself. This is the ultimate intention of these practices.

Practices 1 through 5 form what we are calling the Core Practices. These five practices can constitute a complete spiritual practice, which becomes the foundation for everything we do. The second five practices are called the Special Practices. They are refinements and special applications of the Core Practices.

## Special Practices

Practices 6 through 10 are specialized practices that have a more specific focus. These practices are meant to be engaged for a limited period of time. Some of these are self-focused, some are other-focused, and some are a combination. Initially, you should do these in the order presented. After completing all five, you may then pick and choose certain ones to do again.

The special practices consist of temporarily viewing your life experience through a particular lens. Each practice utilizes a different lens. Each lens is not taken to be true in an absolute sense. *We simply accept it as being true for the period of our practice.* It is important that we not get lost in a philosophical debate as to whether or not a particular lens is really true, because this will detract from our practice and the potential benefits derived from it. For example, with Practice 6 (Everything Is My Teacher), do not become embroiled in an internal or external debate about "whether or not this is really the truth." Similarly, when you engage the practice, don't question its veracity by saying, "How could this person possibly be my teacher ... no way!" Simply accept it as a "given reality" for the designated period of your practice.

The core practices can become permanently incorporated into your everyday life. This is not the intention with the special practices. Let's return to our tennis analogy. In a practice session, you may set up markers on the court as targets for where you try to hit the ball so that you can become skillful at hitting the ball into certain strategic areas, such as the corners or deep in the backcourt. The markers themselves are used only for a short period of time; they are not there during the real game. But the skills you've acquired by doing this will be used every time you play tennis. The same idea applies to our special practices.

After completing each of the special practices, you may choose to return to any one of them and repeat that practice for a fixed period of time. This can be helpful as a way of working with specific issues or challenges that arise in your life. For example, if you are in the midst of a great deal of change or uncertainty, then you may want to return to the practice of Dancing With Chaos. Always remember the five core practices form the foundation for each of the special practices and are implicitly included in each of them.

### The Length and Sequence of Each Practice

I recommend each practice be engaged for a period of 30 days before moving on to the next. It takes time to integrate each practice into your life so that it becomes the "new normal." Spiritual practice moves in the opposite direction of our fast food, button-pushing, mouse-clicking, have-it-now culture. Think of it as cultivating a garden: It takes time, patience, and persistence to acquire the nourishment we seek.

If for some reason you cannot engage each practice for 30 days before moving to the next, then make each practice period as long as possible. The benefits of spiritual practice grow exponentially with the time they are engaged. With the core practices, be sure to incorporate the preceding practices into each new practice you take on. These practices are open-ended; there is no finish point. You can engage them for a lifetime and still continue to experience growth and development.

### Specific Chapter Sections

Each chapter will contain certain sections addressing various aspects of the practice presented. These sections are as follows:
- What Is This Practice?
- Why This Practice Is Transformative
- Forms of the Practice

- Perils on the Path
- FAQ (Frequently Asked Questions)

## What Is This Practice?

In this section I describe in detail exactly what the practice is, and sometimes, what it is *not*. I describe the various facets of the practice and how to implement these into your daily life.

## Why This Practice Is Transformative

In this section, I will explain how it works to dissolve egocentricity and shift the identity toward true nature. At times I may refer to certain psychological, philosophical, or metaphysical principles that are relevant to this practice.

## Forms of the Practice

The focus of this section is the various forms and (sometimes) levels of each practice. Each practice is meant to be actively employed in your everyday life, and some practices can be done in a formal meditation period as well. There may be various levels of skill, effort, or detail relative to a given practice; if so, I will explore each of these. I may also explore specific facets or applications of the practice.

## Perils on the Path

Here I will talk about some of the hindrances and pitfalls present with any spiritual practice. The ego will resist spiritual practice in a variety of ways; some examples are: rationalization, denial, doubt, distraction, and delusion. I will also address hindrances or pitfalls specific to each individual practice.

Every spiritual practice has what may be termed a "far enemy" and a "near enemy." The far enemy is typically the exact opposite of the spiritual practice. For example, if our practice is Deep Self-Acceptance then the far enemy would be some form of resistance such as fear, anger, or judgment. The far enemy is fairly easy to recognize.

The near enemy is much more subtle. It may look a lot like the practice itself. It can masquerade as the practice but still be a subtle form of resistance. For example, apathy or resignation may masquerade as acceptance. The practice of Deep Self-Acceptance is not a resignation to some present condition nor is it apathetically "not caring what happens."

The near enemy can be far more dangerous that the far enemy because it is more difficult to detect. One type of near enemy of transformational practice is that it may unknowingly be used in a translational framework. For example, we may engage the practice of Universal Benevolence while unconsciously holding the hidden intention of receiving some type of payoff or reward. I may believe I am being "more spiritual" if I engage this practice, or I may be unconsciously hoping that others will like me more. When the practice reinforces ego-identification rather than dissolving it, then it undermines our potential for transformation.

In closing, I want to make two important points. First, transformation involves dissolving ego-identification; this does not mean dissolving the ego itself. The ego is simply one's sense of self. It is quite often necessary to have a sense of self in order to function in the world. But when we are exclusively identified with the ego, we are imprisoned in it and we become a slave to its vicissitudes. Transformation means transcending, *and including,* the ego so that it becomes the servant of a higher power—our true self. The ego then becomes more transparent and serves as a vehicle for original nature, rather than an obstruction to it. To live originally is to have a healthy ego, and yet not be limited by our identification with it.

Second, I see no inherent problem with a spiritual practice that does strengthen ego-identification; *as long as you are clear this is your intention, and you are not using it to masquerade as a transformational practice.* A translational practice can help one to feel secure, comfortable, and more in control. Transformational practice can do quite the opposite because it involves a death of the old self and a rebirth into a greater reality. Yet when we live consciously centered in the ever-present origin, we no longer have the need for security, comfort, and control as we once understood these to be.

## FAQ

In this section I address various questions that might arise relative to a specific practice. These are included for deeper clarification and understanding.

# 3. PRACTICE 1:
# RADICAL SELF-AWARENESS

## What Is This Practice?

In the broadest sense of the term, *self-awareness* simply means I am aware of myself as an individual separate and apart from others. When an animal sees itself in a mirror and says, "Hey, that's me!" that's one indication of self-awareness. Virtually all humans have this ability. A few other animal species seem to have it as well.

In a deeper sense of the word, self-awareness means that "I know that I know." I have the ability to reflect upon my own awareness. I am aware not only of a body called *me*, but I am also aware of a sense of an internal *me* looking in the mirror at me as the body. I have an internal mirror that reflects the contents of my mind just as the external mirror reflects the image of my body.

Radical Self-Awareness takes us another layer deeper. As I recognize my physical self in the mirror, and as I am aware of seeing that image, I can also be aware of my reaction to this awareness. I may notice I feel some chagrin at how much gray hair I see in that image staring back at me. (Is that *really* me?) *I am aware of my response to my awareness.* I see an image in the mirror, I recognize that image as me, I have a mental judgment about that image (I'm getting old), and I have an emotional response to that judgment (dismay). I am aware of all this *and* I am aware that I am aware of all this! Welcome to the practice of Radical Self-Awareness!

This practice is to be aware of my present moment experience and to be aware of my mental/emotional/physical response to this experience and to be aware that I am aware of all this. It is easier to do it than to describe it!

The challenge lies in doing it continuously.

We begin the practice by creating the intention to be radically self-aware in each moment. We are *not* creating a goal of 100 percent awareness every minute of every day. This is very unlikely to occur; but that is the direction in which we constantly move.

Returning to our previous tennis analogy, as a beginner I would not expect to perform perfectly every time I played. Even a seasoned professional knows this will not happen; but that is his intention, and it is mine too, even as a beginner. The intention is the ideal toward which we move; it is not a goal we pressure ourselves to achieve. Do not be discouraged if you miss the imagined mark of perfection; just return to your intention.

In the practice of Radical Self-Awareness, we set the intention to be aware of all facets of our experience in each moment. We begin by being aware of our experience in this very moment, whatever it may be. The spiritual teacher Jiddu Krishnamurti tells us, "The first step is the last step. The first step is to perceive, perceive what you are thinking, perceive your ambition, perceive your anxiety, your loneliness, your despair … perceive it without any condemnation, justification, without wishing it to be different."[10] And I would add that even if you do find yourself condemning or justifying, just become aware of that as well, without adding anything to it.

We seem to exist in two parallel worlds: one world that appears to be external to our sense of self and an internal world of thoughts, feelings, and desires, which is much closer to "me." There is yet another sense of *me* that is aware of all this. I can be aware of both my external world and my internal world—and be aware that an "I" is aware of it all.

---

With this self-observation, we see our subjective world of thoughts and emotions is largely an interpretive one. Much of our inner world is preoccupied with interpreting and giving meaning to our external world. This may be likened to TV commentators at a sporting event. One of the commentators describes what is occurring objectively on the playing field, doing the "play-by-play," while the other commentator is analyzing these facts, interpreting them, and giving them some meaning. Often the second commentator will tell a story about one of the players, cite some stats for the listeners, or compare this season with prior years. It is not difficult to see we have both these guys inside us! One of us sees what is and one of us tells us what it means. Radical Self-Awareness is to be aware of both of these "voices" and to be able to differentiate between the two of them.

In your practice you differentiate between your basic experience of seeing, hearing, sensing, and the mind's response to what you've seen, heard, and felt. Learn to separate the content of your (primary) experience from the context (the ascribed meaning) you give to it. This can be accomplished only by direct awareness, not by thinking about it.

When we are unable to separate these two facets of our awareness, they become conflated; we get them mixed up. Our primary experience is then perceived through the lens of our unconscious interpretations. Our objective world is colored by our subjective lens. We then perceive the primary experience *itself* as good or bad based upon our unconscious interpretation of that experience.

To speak metaphorically, imagine you are seeing a garden filled with pink roses, whereas your friend sees them as violet roses. Perhaps you get into an argument over the true color of these roses. Alas, you are unable to resolve the issue until you both practice Radical Self-Awareness, and you discover your eyeglasses have a pink tinge to them, and your friend discovers her glasses have a purple tinge. Then you both remove your glasses and see the roses are white! Upon seeing this, you make up and live happily ever after!

Although I have regarded this topic rather whimsically, the psychology behind it has enormous consequences. Much human suffering has resulted from a lack of this understanding. Many marriages have ended and many wars have been fought over "the color of the roses."

Radical Self-Awareness means being aware of the primary experiences of seeing, hearing, feeling, thinking; and it means being aware of the meaning I give to these experiences. It means being aware of the emotional response that arises from my ascribed meanings, as well as seeing all this without judgment or analysis. This is not as complicated as it sounds; it all happens in an instant. I may not always have the full awareness in the exact instant it arises, but as I reflect back on my emotional reactions, I will begin to see all this unfolding. With practice, I can see this more quickly each time it occurs.

For example, I say "hello" to a friend and she does not acknowledge my greeting. I become aware that I'm feeling angry at her. This can throw me into a story about "how inconsiderate and insensitive this person is" … and so on. Or I can stop and breathe and feel the sensations in my body and pay attention to my feeling of anger. I may discover that beneath the anger lies some hurt feelings. I realize I feel hurt because I believe my friend doesn't value me enough to respond to my greeting. If I stay present to the experience of hurt, I will see it rests upon my interpretation that my friend deliberately ignored me. Seeing this, I understand there are other possible interpretations—perhaps she did not hear me, or she was preoccupied. I may then see how often I base my own sense of worth on the responses (or lack thereof) from others. I can see this without any self-judgment, and may even feel grateful for the insight. All this can occur within a few seconds if I simply take time to be aware of my own experience in the moment.

## Body Awareness

A central part of this practice is to be aware of sensations in the body as continuously as possible. Simply infuse your body with awareness. Feel the body from inside the body itself. We are not just thinking about the body, or attempting to visualize it but simply feeling it directly. Notice whatever sensations naturally come into your awareness. Feel these sensations without interpretation or reactivity.

A simple form of this practice is to just sit for a few minutes and notice the sensations that appear in the body. For example, you may feel the touch of clothing on your skin; the warmth or coolness of the air in the room; a bit of tension in the back; a little tightness in the belly, and so on. That's the basic practice.

Don't experience your body simply as a mental image; instead, feel the body directly from *within* the body. As an experiment, look at your hand for about 10 seconds; notice the mental image of your hand. Then close your eyes, let go of that image, and feel your hand directly. Feel it from the inside of the hand itself. Do this for about 30 seconds. Notice your experience and then contrast it with your visual image of the hand. What is the difference? The direct sensing experience of the hand may not conform at all to the visual image of the same hand!

In this practice, we are not looking for anything in particular. You are not trying to make something happen; you are just noticing what is naturally occurring on its own. Don't try to control, analyze, or interpret anything you feel. Just be aware.

When mental or emotional reactivity arises automatically, just notice this reaction and return your awareness to the primary experience of sensing the body. When there is reactivity of any sort, just notice it occurring and return your focus to the primary experience of feeling sensations in the body. Do not be at all concerned with how often you may seem to become distracted; just keep returning to the practice of body awareness.

## Observing the Mind

Another very important facet of this practice is awareness of mental activity. This form of practice can be challenging at first because we are typically more identified with the mind than with the body. My sense of *me* is partly a physical experience, but it is primarily a mental experience. My sense of self is deeply connected with my desires, emotions, and beliefs. My habituated thinking patterns are driven by this core sense of self.

We do live in a physical world, but we tend to experience life primarily through the world of our beliefs, thoughts, and feelings. We may even believe these thoughts and feelings are an accurate picture of reality itself. We will then use this inner "reality" to interpret the external events and circumstances in our life, and perhaps we will respond to our life circumstances from this interpretation. Sure enough, our world begins to reflect our beliefs about it! We may then use this as "evidence" of the veracity of our internal beliefs, thoughts, and feelings, which reinforces our belief in their accuracy. This is the self-reinforcing cycle by which the egoic-self creates our personal sense of reality.

When we can simply observe the activity of the mind rather than assume our perceptions are eternal truth, we begin to interrupt this self-reinforcing cycle. We can then begin to relate *to* the mind rather than *from* the mind.

The former subject has now become the object of awareness. You could say I am now *looking at* my rose-(or whatever)-colored glasses rather than *looking through* them. I see myself and the world with new eyes. This can be a very liberating experience because I am no longer held hostage by the capricious tyranny of the conditioned mind.

Relate to the mind rather than from it. Be aware of your reactions to life without being embedded in these reactions. Be mindful that you are mad, sad, or glad, but do not become totally identified with these reactive emotions. Don't interpret anything as good or bad; just notice when you are aware and when you are not.

Maintaining some awareness of body sensations is always very important in this process. Experience your emotions and desires primarily as sensations in the body, knowing they are simply conditioned responses to your life circumstances. This allows you to differentiate between physical and mental experience. As you maintain awareness of body sensations, you will begin to experience mental activity with less identification. You can then fully experience your desires and emotions without getting lost in them or compulsively acting them out.

For example, if someone speaks to me and I hear criticism, then I just notice my internal reaction (anger) and deliberately keep my attention on the sensations I feel in the body (tightness in the chest, and so on); I focus attention on my experience in the present moment. I notice my mental/emotional interpretation (*he's mean and stupid*), but do not engage it. I neither believe it nor dispute it. I just see what it is and then bring awareness back to sensations in the body. (Remember to breathe!)

This is not easy to do. The mind may be strongly conditioned to interpret and respond to a given circumstance in some particular (and familiar) way. If I've experienced a lot of criticism as a child, then I may have developed a defensive strategy that responds automatically. It may be anger, shame, hurt, withdrawal, attack, rationalization, and so on. It's very similar to how a computer functions: Click on a certain icon and the program immediately fires up!

As you maintain awareness of physical sensations, you may experience some difficult feelings. It might seem easier to return to the familiar defensive strategy, but if you're willing to stay present to your experience in the body, you will become aware of the underlying wound that was shielded by the conditioned response. Initially this may feel scary and confusing, but as you stay present to the body, you will eventually move through the difficulties and discover that aspect of your authentic self that's been held hostage by the unhealed wound and its related defensive structure. This insight will free you from the need for the defensive response and will reveal the creative power and beauty of the authentic self, which has unlimited awareness and freedom of choice.

Let's summarize this discussion. In the practice of body awareness, the instruction is to feel the body from within the body itself. In the practice of mental awareness, the instruction is to *observe* the activity of the mind. To be an observer is to have some distance between the observer (you) and the observed (mind activity). We deliberately disidentify from mental activity via the process of observation because we are usually deeply identified with mental activity.

Desires, emotions, and beliefs may be likened to stars that have strong gravitational fields. Some of them can feel like black holes, powerful enough to consume us if we get too close! If we're drifting through space, we're vulnerable to these gravitational fields, but if we are standing on the earth, we can safely observe these big stars. Body awareness provides us with solid ground to stand on as we observe these powerful mental objects.

Be very patient with yourself in this process because identification with the mind is very deep. It's easy to get tangled up in judgments of "doing it right" or "making progress." If this occurs then see that this is just another conditioned mental pattern; don't take it personally. Simply return awareness to physical sensations—this will always bring you back to the present moment.

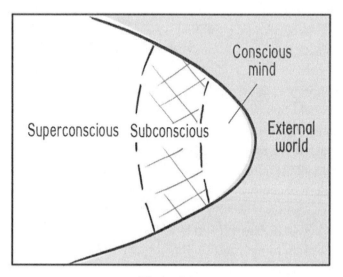

**Figure 3-1**

### Why This Practice Is Transformative

Charles Fillmore, the cofounder of Unity, presents a model of the psyche that is useful for our discussion. (See Fig. 3-1) In *Dynamics for Living*, he writes:

> The subconscious is the vast, silent realm that lies back of the conscious mind and between it and the superconscious. It may be called the sensitive place of mind. Its true office is to receive impressions from the superconsciousness and to reproduce them upon the canvas of the conscious mind.
>
> Man, however, having lost the consciousness of the indwelling Father as an ever-present reality, has reversed the process and impresses the subconscious

from the conscious mind. In this way the former is made to register impressions according to the thought held in conscious mind at the time the impression is made.[11]

In the Fillmore model, the conscious level of mind perceives and relates to the external world. Beneath this level, below the level of consciousness, lies the subconscious mind. This is sometimes called the storehouse mind; it is where all our memories reside. Beyond the subconscious level is the superconscious level of mind, which has constant access to the ever-present origin.[12]

The vast majority of humanity is unaware of the superconscious mind. This lack of awareness creates a sense of deficiency within the subconsciousness. Seemingly detached from the origin of all love, wisdom, and power, we subconsciously feel fear, lack, and limitation. In the conscious awareness, we may experience this as a vague sense of emptiness or deficiency, and perhaps a chronic sense of dissatisfaction. In this condition, we attempt to alleviate this feeling of dissatisfaction by moving outward, toward the external world. We look for the external world to provide us that which seems to be lacking internally.

As children we develop a strategy for finding external fulfillment for these internal deficiency needs. As we mature, this strategy becomes deeply embedded in the subconscious. We automatically seek some object, person, activity, social role, or title to fill the inner emptiness we experience. This strategy is doomed to fail.

Our strategy is doomed to fail for two reasons. First, the external world is incapable of filling an internal need that can be filled only through conscious awareness of the superconscious. Second, the subconscious mind projects its own unmet needs onto the external world. The deficiency we feel inside is projected onto the external world, as is the assumed fulfillment of that deficiency. To the conscious awareness, the world has that which we urgently need, but the world also appears to contain that which prevents us from getting what we need. Thus we see a fractured world; a world that is filled with conflict. We see a world filled with good and evil, friends and enemies, angels and demons. We see the world not as *it is* but as *we are*.

For example, if I feel disconnected from the superconscious—the ultimate source of my love—then I will feel a deficiency of love within me. If I am unable to see the true cause of my deficiency (which is very likely), then the ego will project both the cause of my deficiency and its fulfillment onto someone or something in the world. I am seeing both the cause of my problem *and* its solution as outside of myself. I will see the world filled with persons or objects (or persons *as* objects) that seem to be able to fill my inner need or able to frustrate its fulfillment. And, just to thicken the plot, if and when I do acquire the relationship or circumstance of my dreams, it will ultimately be found to be wanting, because it is never able of fill my internal emptiness. And perhaps I will go on, in search of another ... and another and ...

In the practice of Radical Self-Awareness, we attempt to meet the external world with a clear mind so we can function effectively in our everyday life. At the same time we direct some of our attention to the internal world of physical sensations, thoughts, emotions, and desires. We notice our internal responses to external events. We become every bit as interested in our internal world as we are in our external world.

As we do this practice skillfully over time, several things will begin to occur. First, we gradually cease to project our subconscious deficiencies, desires, and conflicts onto the external world. We will begin to see the external world more clearly and realistically; we see it as it is rather than as we are.

Second, we become more aware of the previously ignored contents of the subconscious, which was formerly projected onto the world. This is the most difficult part because we will see and feel those subconscious contents we have been running from; we face our hidden fears and we feel our buried feelings. Painful though it is, it is a pain that heals. The pain that heals is usually poignant, but temporary; as opposed to the pain of resistance that is dull and persistent.

Third, we become more directly aware of the presence of the superconscious as we turn toward it. We see the ultimate source of all we desire is from within us. We will begin to experience periods of deep peace and satisfaction that are unconditional; we see true happiness is not dependent upon our life circumstances.

We see the world and the people in it in a more realistic and creative way. No longer seeing the world as a place that can save or destroy us, we see it as a field for our creative expression. Within ourselves, we begin to experience both the light and the shadows more intensely. We see the shadows more clearly because the subconscious reveals itself more openly to awareness. As the shadows of the subconscious dissipate under the light of consciousness, we gaze more clearly into the light of the superconscious. We experience it becoming ever-brighter, we become infused with this light, and *we see that we are the light itself*. This light then shines through us into the external world. We are in the world, but not of it; we are living originally.

## Forms of Awareness Practice

The two basic forms of Radical Self-Awareness practice are the general practice and the formal practice. The general form is practiced in the midst of your everyday life activities. Let's talk about this one first.

We begin with the general intention to be aware at all times. Since this is fairly difficult to do, you may find it can be helpful to employ a particular strategy. Certain daily activities may be more amenable to awareness practice than others. For most of us, it is easier to do the practice when alone than with other people. It is easier to do the practice when engaged in fairly routine tasks. Simple chores such as personal hygiene activities, housecleaning, and yard work are great opportunities to engage the practice.

A related strategy is to engage the practice continuously for the first hour of each day. During this period, we are typically engaged in relatively routine activities and perhaps we are alone. Start out by simply focusing on body sensations as you perform your morning routine. If possible, move a bit more slowly and deliberately in order to enhance the awareness practice.

At other times during the day, even if we are quite busy, we often have brief "down times" such as waiting at a stoplight or standing in line at the store. These are great opportunities to engage in a brief awareness practice. Simply take a deep breath and feel the sensations in your body; be fully present to your experience of life, even if it's only for a few seconds.

As you engage in the more complex mental or emotional activities of your day, you can still engage the practice; perhaps it's to a lesser degree, but any amount of awareness is better than none at all! My personal strategy is to try to maintain continuous awareness of my hands whenever I am sitting down and to maintain awareness of my feet when I am standing or walking. (This has some very practical benefits as well—I am less likely to lose things or trip over something when I am mindful!)

Even during times of intense emotional interactions with others, it can enhance our ability to relate consciously and compassionately to them if we can stay present to our physical sensations. We are less likely to "get lost in the fray" when we have some connection to our present moment experience in the body.

Awareness while eating can make a big difference in the quality, and perhaps the quantity, of our meal. A primary recovery tool for compulsive overeaters is to eat with awareness. As you consume your meal, become very aware of the taste of the food as well as the physical sensations and emotions that arise as you eat slowly and mindfully.

Eventually, you may develop the ability to keep part of your total awareness on body sensations throughout the day. You can be aware of the body while you are walking, talking, reading, writing, and working. It takes a bit of practice, but it is well worth the effort; the practical benefits of living consciously can be enormous. Life works better when we are present to it. Try it and you will see for yourself!

### Formal Practice

Let's talk about the formal awareness practice. Although the primary practice is in our everyday life, a period of daily sitting meditation is also essential. In the sitting periods we sharpen our practice by focusing clearly on some small part of our total experience. Typically, we begin by concentrating on the breath: We focus on the breath and then return awareness to the breath each time the attention wanders. This concentration practice helps us to disengage from the habituated thought processes that continuously reinforce the ego structure. After being with the breath for a while, bring your awareness into the body. Feel the sensations that arise in the body as you sit quietly. Your attention will wander at times, but when you notice this, simply return your attention to your body.

As you bring awareness into the body, you may also notice emotions and desires arising. If so, just notice these without either resisting or indulging them. Stay primarily with the body sensations and notice how these sensations may change as you bring a gentle and consistent awareness to them. The intention is to be fully present to each experience as it arises, feeling the body sensations, noticing thoughts and emotions, but not resisting or getting lost in any of it.

Practice consistently. Daily sitting practice is very important, even if it is for only five or 10 minutes a day. This daily sitting practice reinforces your intention to awaken from the egocentric trance in which we live much of our life. Practicing even a few minutes a day is far better than not at all. However, it works much better if you can extend your practice to 20 minutes or more each day. It takes a while to disengage from the momentum of habituated thought processes and settle into direct awareness of your present moment experience.

It can be very helpful to be part of a weekly or biweekly meditation group. It is very helpful to have a support group of peers who are also committed to a transformational awareness practice. The backbone of the very successful Twelve-Step recovery movement is the regular group meetings. It is axiomatic in that movement that if you want to recover, then you "keep coming back" to the meetings. Our awareness practice is also part of a recovery movement; perhaps we could call it "humans anonymous." The purpose of this movement is recovery from our addiction to egocentricity—which is endemic among human beings!

Periodically attending a meditation retreat can also be very helpful. At these retreats, you are able to take your practice much deeper than in your daily practice. It is very helpful to temporarily let go of your routine activities and immerse yourself in a long period of dedicated practice.

The daily sitting practice, your during-the-day practice, the weekly gatherings, and the occasional retreats will form a powerful and systematic way to engage your transformative practice of Radical Self-Awareness.

## Perils on the Path

Each spiritual practice has both a far enemy and a near enemy. The far enemy of a practice is usually something that is exactly the opposite of the practice itself. The far enemy of Radical Self-Awareness is unconsciousness, spacing out, going on "autopilot." When this happens, we want to wake up as soon as possible. This is why creating a clear intention is so important; a strong intention will help us to wake up. As the compass needle that guides the direction of our practice, our intention will help us see when we have veered off course. (An important part of this practice is to often remind ourselves of our intention.) This is one reason why the daily practice of formal meditation is very important—it reinforces our intention to be awake. This is why having a support group is also very important. The group can help us see when we have strayed from the course and can help to reaffirm our intention.

With transformational practice, the greatest peril is to unwittingly feed the ego-identification when we think we are dissolving it. Be on the alert for this near enemy; it appears like spiritual practice but it is a counterfeit. This near enemy may be more dangerous than the far enemy because it is more difficult to recognize; it masquerades as the real thing. It is like a computer virus; invisible, but silently working to undermine our true intention.

There may be several near enemies to Radical Self-Awareness. Perhaps the most common is that of self-improvement. Now what can be wrong with self-improvement? Is it not laudable to want to better oneself? The answer is that there is nothing at all wrong with self-improvement; it is laudable to want to improve yourself. But the intention of this practice is transformation, not self-improvement. We are not seeking a new and improved version of the old self. We are seeking something beyond the present level of our understanding; that's what transformation is all about. Self-improvement has a goal, an agenda. Transformation is letting go of all agendas and standing in naked reality. Holding the intention for transformation is not the same as trying to achieve a goal. There is no "finish line." We have no "prize" imaged in the back of our mind. Our intention is to radically be what we already are—but don't know it!

How do we spot this near enemy? A good place to start is to be on the lookout for any sense of trying to "get somewhere" with your practice. Notice any sense of frustration when it feels like you are not "making progress." Notice any sense of pride that arises when it feels like you are "making progress." Watch for judgments or comparisons of self with others. Frustration and judgments may be signs of hidden expectations. Watch for hidden expectations of "growth" or "progress."

Another potential peril on the path is doubt. Now, doubt itself can be skillful when employed wisely. A skillful form of doubt is when we doubt the veracity of what the world tells us. This doesn't mean becoming a cynic, but it does mean not blindly taking as truth that which you have not directly experienced yourself. This form of doubt may be useful.

Doubt becomes a peril when you lose faith in yourself and in the practice. This type of doubt can undermine your practice; it can even bring it to a complete halt. Doubt will often arise when we have hidden expectations. I have heard students say, "I have been doing this practice for a long time and it doesn't seem to be doing any good."

> My response is, "What would 'doing any good' look like?"
>
> "Well ... I don't feel any better than I used to."

"Aha! So you're expecting to feel better as a result of this practice?"

"Well … Yes, I guess so."

"That's not the right intention for this practice!"

Our hidden assumptions can run very deep; and they can undermine our practice if we are not alert.

What should you do when you discover the near enemy? The specific answer will depend upon your exact circumstance, but in general, *simply be aware of it*. Just see it and continue the practice of being present to your experience in this very moment. Seeing the hindrance and not judging it is the best way to become free from it.

It is also helpful to remind yourself that the intention of transformational practice is to go deeper into your present experience so you can discover a greater reality hidden within it.

## FAQ

**1. Can't a spiritual practice be both transformative and translative? Does it really have to be one or the other?**

As I am using these terms, they describe different intentions for spiritual practice; they point in different directions. In a translational practice, we intend to make the ego more functional and more comfortable. In a transformative practice, we intend to disidentify from the ego and to discover a larger self beyond it. These two intentions seem to be mutually exclusive.

But transformation does not mean we lose our ego; we simply lose our primary identification with it. The ego will then serve as a vehicle for the higher self. As a vehicle for the higher self, the ego becomes much more functional than when we're exclusively identified with it.

Also, many of the goals desired in the translative practices may come into fruition with transformative practice. However, these are always seen as by-products (they are never the primary intention of the practice). A common example is that of physical or emotional healing, which is often a by-product of transformational practice.

**2. Living in the present moment is fine, but there are times when I do have to make plans for the future.**

Certainly; the awareness practice is not dependent upon what you are doing or feeling or thinking; it is simply being fully aware to your present moment experience, *whatever it is*. If you are thinking about the past or the future, you can be aware *in the present moment* that you are thinking about the past and the future. The thinking itself is taking place in the present moment, no matter what you are thinking about. Awareness always takes place in the present moment.

**3. I have to live in the world; this requires interpretation and giving meaning to what I see and hear.**

Yes, it does. There is nothing at all wrong with interpreting your experiences and giving them some meaning; in fact, you cannot do otherwise, because interpretation occurs automatically. The important question is, "Am I aware that I am giving this meaning to the experience that I am having?" If I know I am giving my experience a particular meaning, I can decide if that interpretation is accurate or helpful. If it isn't, then I can change it. If I don't know I am assigning this meaning to an experience, then I will believe my ascribed meaning is part of objective reality. Then I have no choice or freedom to change my interpretation; I will simply believe "this is the way it is." Then I'm living in delusion, and I will eventually crash headlong into reality!

Listen to or download the audio meditation for this
practice at *unitybooks.org/living*.

# 4. PRACTICE 2:
# DEEP SELF-ACCEPTANCE

In our common usage of the term, *self-acceptance* means I have a self-image I find to be acceptable, and perhaps even likeable: *I like this person I take myself to be.* The internal image of "who I am" is consistent with my image of an ideal self—or at least, a "good-enough" self.

Perhaps I feel competent at my work, I believe I am a good father, and I have some status in my community, so I feel good about myself.

This assessment of my being "okay" is based upon standards inherited from my family and my culture. This form of self-acceptance is relative and is conditional; my sense of self is defined relative to others and to external standards, and my self-acceptance is dependent upon maintaining the conditions of acceptance, such as competency or intelligence. If I no longer meet these conditions, my self-acceptance goes out the window.

## What Is This Practice?

The practice of Deep Self-Acceptance has nothing to do with any particular self-image, and it is not about comparing myself against any ideal or standard. Deep Self-Acceptance is simply the unconditional acceptance of my present moment experience, whatever that experience may be. The "self" I accept is simply the sense of self I experience each and every moment. This self is not an image but rather a felt experience.

Self is not only a stream of experience, but it is also *that which is aware of each experience*. I am an ever-changing stream of experiences, and I am the unchanging witness of that stream. If I were to say "I am sad," then who I am is the experience of sadness as well as that which is aware of the sadness. The sadness will eventually morph into some other experience, but that which is aware of the sadness does not change.

Deep Self-Acceptance is simply allowing each experience to be what it is without interfering in any way. I am fully present to each experience without any resistance, analysis, interpretation, manipulation, or control. I experience "just what is here" and add nothing to it. I experience each sensation, emotion, and thought completely, and then I let it go. To use a campfire metaphor: I don't attempt to extinguish the fire, but I don't throw any more wood onto it either. I just let the fire burn until it burns itself out.

I begin the practice by creating the intention of deep acceptance and I return to that intention quite often. Yet I know at times I will automatically react, resist, judge, or interpret my present experience, in spite of my intention. This is not a problem. I simply notice whatever arises automatically (Radical Self-Awareness). I allow it to arise and add nothing to what has already arisen. Even if I have unwittingly "thrown a log" onto the fire, I stop doing so as soon as I become aware of it. Even if I am unconsciously engaged in an orgy of judgment and criticism, as soon as I become aware, I simply return to the present moment without further criticism of myself or anyone else. I breathe and I sense my body. I do not judge the judgments or resist the resistance.

I want to emphasize that I am referring to my *internal* experiences, not necessarily to my words or actions. At times it *is* necessary to control my words and my actions. Acceptance of an internal experience does *not* mean acting out these internal feelings in an unconscious or harmful manner. I can accept the physical sensations, thoughts, and emotions without acting any of it out.

## What This Practice Is Not

Internally, I allow everything to arise naturally. Externally, I act ethically and responsibly to the best of my ability. I can completely accept an emotion or a desire and yet refrain from acting upon this. Deep acceptance means accepting my present internal experience completely *and* acting ethically and responsibly in the world. And, if I do speak or act irresponsibly, I simply acknowledge this and make any necessary amends.

If I am engaged in a harmful addiction or compulsive behavior, my spiritual practice may need to include a program such as psychotherapy or a Twelve-Step recovery group. Deep Self-Acceptance can be practiced at all times and under any conditions, but it may need to be augmented by other types of practice.

Deep acceptance does not mean I believe my perceptions are absolutely right or superior to other perspectives. I don't use this practice to justify self-righteous anger or to make someone wrong. I can fully embrace my viewpoint and believe it is valid, and yet know another equally valid viewpoint may exist. I also know I may very well see things differently in the future.

In this practice I am less concerned with being right than I am with becoming transformed. It is very helpful to remind myself of this whenever I become attached to a particular viewpoint. If this happens, then I simply breathe and become aware of my present moment experience. When I am strongly attached to something, I may notice there is some internal experience I am resisting. Can I then open up to it, and allow it to arise, without judgment?

Deep Self-Acceptance does not mean I enjoy every experience that arises. I may feel very uncomfortable in this present experience. Acceptance is not the same as liking something. Few of us enjoy pain and discomfort, but these can be experienced without resistance or judgment. I have found pain and discomfort will tend to diminish when I am willing to experience it without resistance. It may take some practice and strong intention, but it is very possible to accept any discomfort without reactivity and judgment. Discomfort is simply discomfort; we don't need to create an "ain't it awful" story about it.

Conversely, I can experience pleasure without becoming addicted to it. I can fully enjoy my present experience without creating a strategy of how to hold on to it or to re-create it. The desire to hold on to it or to re-create it arises from the fear that it will never return; and that fear itself will diminish my experience of pleasure. Think of the person on vacation who is so obsessed with taking pictures and collecting souvenirs that he never truly enjoys the vacation itself! I will enjoy pleasure the most when I am not attached to it.

Radical acceptance is not an attempt to live some idealized image of calmness and serenity. I am not trying to find some "correct" or "perfect" response to my life experiences. I simply respond as I do and then I am aware of and accepting of that response. If I am unclear about taking action in the world then, if possible, I refrain from acting. At times it may be helpful to simply verbalize my internal experience, without any blame or criticism. This level of honesty can be very impactful in our relationship with others. I have found this will often deepen the level of intimacy and trust with another person. But, it does require some willingness to be vulnerable; I have no control over how others may respond to my openness. It may connect us more deeply, or it may frighten them away.

The practice begins with awareness of the present moment experience. With awareness comes choice. One choice is radical acceptance. I can let go of "chasing the story" that may automatically arise in response to certain experiences. I don't need to replay a familiar story such as "I am not good enough" or "people are not trustworthy." If I am aware of chasing the story, then I can choose to let it go and return to my present moment awareness.

## What About Taking Action?

Radical acceptance does not mean I never take action to bring about a change in my life circumstances. Obviously, we all need to make choices and to take action to function in our world. But my primary focus is on the internal experiences that motivate my actions.

Let's make an important distinction between *reacting* and *responding*. A reaction is an automatic response to some internal or external stimulus. I have relatively little control over my internal reactions; they seem to arise very quickly. But I can have more control over my speech and actions. When I am not aware of my experience in the moment, I will tend to (re)act automatically.

With awareness, I can choose to respond rather than react. To respond rather than to react is to speak and act consciously and intentionally. I have the ability to choose my words and actions. I can align that choice with my deepest intention.

As I gain greater awareness and acceptance of my internal experiences, I can become clearer on the intention behind my words and actions. The more clear and conscious I am, the more I am responding to my deepest needs rather than my conditioned desires. As I listen to my deeper needs, I find my life's options will increase and I am less conflicted with others and with my life circumstances.

We all have the same basic needs; safety, love, autonomy, and creativity are some examples. There is a multiplicity of ways these needs can be met for each of us. But our conditioning often tells us these needs can be met only in certain ways. We might hear an internal voice that says, "If he really loved me, he wouldn't do that." Because we all have different conditioning, this can create tremendous difficulties in our relationships.

If we are aware of the deeper need behind the conditioned desire (What I really want is to feel loved …), we see an abundance of options available to us. Not addicted to our need being met in a specific way, we can be flexible, yet intentional, in our relationships with others.

When I am unaware of, or resistant to, my present moment experience, I am much more likely to act out of my conditioned reaction. This often causes suffering for me and for others. As I practice radical awareness and deep acceptance, I become more aware of my thoughts, emotions, and sensations as they arise. This awareness gives me the choice to consciously choose to respond with intention rather than to react unconsciously.

There is wisdom within each of us that knows how to respond perfectly to every life circumstance. Allow that wisdom to emerge. Initially, you may feel a bit awkward or vulnerable when you do not react in a familiar way. Just breathe and stay present to the sensations and the emotions in your body. Eventually, you will feel more at ease with temporarily not knowing what to say or do. To the extent you can stay open and present to the experience of vulnerability, you will open the door for higher wisdom to emerge.

As I become conscious of my deep desires and intentions without attachment to specific outcomes, I begin to see creative new ways these desires can be met with much less stress in my life. The practice of greater awareness and acceptance may seem challenging in the early stages, but it's an investment that's worth its weight in gold, a thousand times over. Infinitely more satisfying than the egocentric desire to "have it my way" is living from your deepest intention and your highest wisdom without attachment to outcome. This is living originally.

At age 15, Rachel Naomi Remen was diagnosed with Crohn's disease. She reacted to the illness and the resultant suffering and limitation with deep resentment. She needed to consult with her disease in the simplest of matters. Would it let me eat this piece of cheese? Would it let me walk up this flight of stairs? She hated her body and she hated her life.

As a young adult, she was walking the beach one day as she found herself comparing her life with that of friends and colleagues of similar age, who seemed to have perfect health and boundless vitality. Her seething resentment erupted into an explosive rage; she allowed herself to feel this rage fully for the first time. As she screamed and felt the rage pulsing through her body, she had a profound insight. The rage was her will to live! The rage was her love for life expressing itself. She saw that at the core of her being, she had an intense love of life. She touched something deep within herself.

Experiencing a deep acceptance of the rage, which had been simmering within her, she found the rage transformed into vitality and a love for life itself. For the first time in her adult life, she was no longer a victim of her disease; she found a new life. Rachel went on to become a medical doctor and an author who has transformed the lives of many people.[13]

### Why This Practice Is Transformative

It is very important to see how we resist our present moment experiences. Ultimately, it is this resistance that blocks our access to the superconsciousness. Referencing the Fillmore model (Fig. 3-1), we see the subconscious lies between conscious awareness and superconsciousness. We can think of resistance as something that "freezes" the memories, desires, and emotions in the subconscious. In this frozen state, they block the light of the superconscious. Acceptance melts this resistance and allows the contents of the subconscious to flow into conscious awareness, where they can be examined, integrated, and released. By fully accepting the subconscious as it reveals itself in the practice of self-awareness, we are dissolving the obscurations which block our access to superconsciousness.

The moment I see and accept my experience of resistance, I have taken a giant step toward dissolving it. Using the term "unity consciousness" to describe superconscious awareness, author Ken Wilber explains it this way:

> ... until you see precisely how you resist unity consciousness, all your efforts to "achieve" it will be in vain, because what we are trying to achieve is also what we are unconsciously resisting and trying to prevent ... And that understanding itself might allow a glimpse of unity consciousness, *for that which sees resistance is itself free of resistance.*[14]

With deep acceptance, I see the "I" that is aware of resistance is itself free of resistance. Rather than being negatively identified with the resistance, deep acceptance allows me to see it clearly *and thus see it is not truly me.* Identity then shifts from the object (resistance) to the subject (witness) and I realize the witness itself (I am) is free of resistance!

As I become more accepting of each experience, my awareness opens into greater clarity and more freedom of choice. As the storm clouds from the subconscious pass through my awareness without resistance, I have clearer access to the sunlight of the superconscious. My present awareness is less contaminated by the subconscious, and it becomes more infused with the clear light of superconsciousness.

As I relax into each experience with deep acceptance, I begin to see my external life will reflect the experience of nonresistance. I am no longer bracing myself against a threatening world; I begin to move with the flow of life rather than struggle against it. With radical awareness, I gain the clarity to function in the world more skillfully; with deep acceptance, I gain the confidence to live in the world with greater ease and a sense of well-being.

## Forms of the Practice

Deep acceptance has a general and a formal practice; each has its advantages. The general practice is for everyday life. It is here I have the best opportunity to experience resistance as it arises in its various forms. Rather than seeing this resistance as a problem, I can see it as an opportunity to deepen my practice. Awareness of resistance is always an opening for transformation.

I can accept some of my experiences only by seeing how I am *not* accepting them. Much of my resistance is subconscious. I may be totally unaware of it until some life event or circumstance triggers it. Practicing Radical Self-Awareness, I can see resistance as it arises, without believing in it or acting it out. Once I am aware of it, I can then choose how to respond to it.

For example, I hear a remark I interpret as criticism; I feel anger beginning to arise. Without self-awareness, I might respond by lashing out or by sinking into depression. Neither of these is a skillful response. With self-awareness, I can see the anger as it arises and then choose how to respond to this experience. I breathe, I feel the sensations in my body, and I notice thoughts and emotions. With some clarity, I can then choose to ask the other person what they meant, ignore the remark, or talk to my psychotherapist; my options are virtually unlimited. Without self-awareness, I have no options; I react blindly.

Resistance takes on one of two general forms. One is of *aversion*.

Aversion is an active form of resistance. Fear and anger are manifestations of aversion. It can appear in a variety of other forms. It may show up as condemnatory judgment, as rationalization, as denial, or as projection. It may be experienced physically in the form of tension in some part of the body. If a sensation, emotion, or desire seems unbearable or unacceptable, I may resist it by unconsciously tensing certain muscles in my body.

Most of us have had the experience of feeling anger welling up and then feeling tightening in the jaw and constriction of the breath; we may feel tension in the arms and shoulders and hardening of facial muscles. We might have these sensations even without the awareness of being angry. This is fairly common for adults, but is quite rare for a 3-year-old. If a toddler becomes angry, he simply expresses himself with tears and a temper tantrum. As we grow older, we learn to control our feelings by holding them in the body. Eventually this becomes automatic; we don't even know we are doing it.

Practicing self-awareness and self-acceptance will allow us to see how often resistance arises. It's very important not to see this as a mistake or a problem, because this will shut us down even more. See the awareness of resistance as an opportunity for freedom and transformation. But it doesn't come cheaply; we must be willing to experience the underlying pain or anxiety buried beneath the resistance.

Resistance can also manifest as craving or addiction; the mind looks outward to avoid looking inward. Resistance is the fuel that feeds obsessive thinking and compulsive behavior. If we are resisting an inner experience, we may be driven toward an external object in an attempt to assuage our discomfort. Behind every compulsion is some form of internal resistance.

As an example, let's say I am obsessed with having the love or the approval of a certain individual. If I take my attention off the object of my obsession and directly experience my sensations and emotions, I may very well find feelings of loneliness or sadness arising. As I open up and allow this experience to deepen, I may have recollections from the past: perhaps some unresolved grief or memories from childhood. I can then see how I came to believe love or approval from this person will make up for what was missing in my past. But it won't. As I open up to allow the hidden pain to be experienced, I will become free of the obsession.

Simple desire is not the same as craving. Some desires are needed for the health of the body and the mind. If I am hungry, I will have a desire for food—perhaps a strong desire; and yet it is not the same as when I am craving chocolate! One is calling for healthy maintenance of the body; the other is (most likely) an attempt to relieve some emotional distress.

A need is a universal human desire. Hunger is an example. Healthy hunger allows a wide variety of food options to satisfy the body's need. Food obsessions have a much more exclusive target; there is little room for choice: A chocolate craving can be filled only with chocolate—and perhaps only a certain kind of chocolate!

I have used food as an example here, but you can substitute the word *food* with gambling, relationships, emotions, social identities, power, knowledge, and so on. The dynamics are essentially the same. Craving is seeking an external fix for a feeling of internal deficiency. In this practice, I hold the intention to refrain from compulsively acting out this craving. If necessary, I will seek a support group to help me become free of compulsive behavior.

In the general practice, I simply live my ordinary life, but in an extraordinary way. I endeavor to live ethically and responsibly with a clear mind and an open heart. I live with awareness and acceptance of each internal experience, and I notice craving or aversion as it arises. I hold the intention to not act out my craving or aversion, but even if I do, I continue the practice right where I am—everything is grist for the mill. *No experience is outside my practice.*

In the formal practice, I sit quietly for a designated period with awareness on the breath and sensations in the body. Here I have the opportunity to see more clearly ways I resist my present moment experience: compulsive thinking, daydreaming, sleepiness, planning, ruminating, and on and on! Seeing resistance, staying present to it, opening and allowing each experience to arise, with acceptance, is the key to this practice. As we gain greater clarity, we see an opportunity to respond to our experiences in a very different way. We see we can open, allow, and relax into what is—moment by moment.

## Perils on the Path

Let's continue this discussion of *far enemy* and *near enemy*. The far enemy is most easy to identify because it is the direct opposite of our practice. The far enemy of deep acceptance is resistance. Resistance can appear as aversion or craving. As aversion, it can show up as anger, judgment, fear, tension, numbness, denial, and other ways. When I'm in aversion, my attitude toward my present life experience is "Go away!" Experiencing aversion, I feel like something is "bad" or "wrong." I am thinking, "Life should not be this way!"

Aversion is not the same as simply saying *"no"* to someone or something. In life, we must make choices, and we need to set limits. Seeing a circumstance that needs correction is not in itself an aversion. To see that something (or someone) is problematic is not necessarily the same as condemning it. We function much more effectively when we objectively identify a problem without condemning it.

Resistance can also appear in the form of craving. It can manifest as addictiveness or compulsiveness, as neediness or dependency. Internally, it feels like deficiency or emptiness. Craving can be very subtle and seductive; it's often harder to see than aversion. It can convince me I cannot live without something or someone. Craving can masquerade as normal desire.

As humans, we do have desires necessary for well-being; we typically call these *needs* or *drives*. As children, we are dependent upon others to get most of our needs met; as adults, much less so. If our needs were adequately met as children, as adults these needs are less problematic, and we will have more skill to acquire what we need because we can see the world with the eyes of an adult rather than as a needy child.

If some needs were chronically unmet when we were children, then they may continue to feel chronically unmet even when we are adults. Having these needs met as an adult does not always make up for the deficiency experienced as a child. These needs can appear insatiable because they cannot be filled externally; and they can be the source of an addiction.

Much of our craving (and aversion) is driven by our unhealed wounds and developmental deficiencies. When I can fully accept this craving without acting upon it (except as necessary to maintain health), I will likely experience the anger and grief of the unmet needs from my childhood. This is not easy to feel, but if I continue the practice of deep acceptance, I will see this grieving is the key to healing the wounds. The healing is in the feeling. As the old wound is healed, I can see the adult need through adult eyes and make wiser choices.

The near enemy of any practice is more difficult to identify because it can masquerade as the practice itself. The near enemy of acceptance can take several forms. One form is denial. I may think I am accepting my present experience when I am not actually experiencing it at all!

Denial can take the form of "spaciness" or numbing out. This can have an anesthetizing effect that superficially looks like acceptance and peace.

I often refer to this as "the counterfeit Buddha." It is true that deep acceptance can bring a state of profound inner peace, but true inner peace is grounded in present moment awareness—it is not a vacuous spaciness.

True peace cannot be judged by external appearances; it can appear in many forms. When true peace is present, we aren't concerned with presenting a particular image to the world.

Another subtle form of resistance is bargaining, which often goes like this: "I will accept this experience so it will go away!" It has a hidden agenda. It's somewhat like giving a dollar to a beggar to "get him off our back" rather than giving from a genuine feeling of charity. Genuine acceptance is unconditional; it has no hidden agenda.

Another peril with this practice is to mix up the internal and external dimensions of the practice. We can substitute external acceptance for internal acceptance. We can practice being passive or nonresistant in an outer way rather than internally. That is not what this practice is.

We always begin with the internal acceptance of sensations, emotions, and thoughts. But this does not automatically mean we accept every *external* condition. We may or may not act in response to our outer circumstances. There are no absolute rules; every circumstance is different. Sometimes we speak up, sometimes we stay silent. Sometimes we take action, sometimes we don't.

It is very important that when we do speak up or take action, it is a response arising from our authentic self rather than a reaction triggered by craving or aversion. As we practice deep acceptance, the needed action (or nonaction) will arise spontaneously from our authentic nature. Initially we may experience a feeling of vulnerability or awkwardness because we are no longer resorting to the familiar strategies. As we continue the practice, this will gradually dissolve. We learn to be in the world in a very different way; we begin to live originally.

## FAQ

**1. What about my negative self-defeating thoughts? Shouldn't I try to change these?**

Perhaps you should, but don't be motivated by an aversive reaction to them. Condemning a negative thought is like trying to extinguish a fire by throwing gasoline on it. Change occurs when we make new choices. You make a genuinely new choice only when you are aware of and nonresistant to what is present right now. If you are in resistance, you are not free to make new choices because you are negatively attached to what is now occurring. Resistance and reactivity negates the power of choice; acceptance empowers you to make new choices.

Remember that acceptance does not mean you necessarily believe every thought that crosses your mind. And it doesn't mean you are clinging to your present experience; it simply means you are not pushing it away. You are not demanding it be other than what it is. Accept what is here in the present moment, and then in the next moment, you are free to make new choices.

**2. If I am not looking for progress or benefits from the practice, how do I know if I am doing it right?**

This is an important question; and this is one reason why it is helpful to have a teacher/mentor and/or support group. There are great benefits to this practice at the physical, mental, and emotional levels, but these are de-emphasized because the real benefit is not experienced within the usual context of "getting better." What we often look for in spiritual practice is a way to feel better. This usually means having less pain and more pleasant experiences. This practice does not always make us feel better in the usual sense of the word.

To attempt to describe the benefit of the practice in words is like trying to describe the taste of a strawberry to someone who has never tasted one. All we can say is, "Let's find one so you can taste it for yourself."

Perhaps the best way to describe it is to say that, as we live closer to reality, it has its own rewards that are clear and unmistakable—but difficult to describe. We will begin to see the difference between pleasure and happiness, between pain and suffering. We may not always experience more pleasure and less pain as a result of this practice, but ultimately we do experience less suffering and more true happiness. You will recognize it as you proceed.

### 3. I don't hear you talking about God. How can you call this a spiritual practice?

In the West we are conditioned to think of *God* and *spirituality* as apart from and beyond the world of our everyday life. I do not make that assumption. I use the term *spirituality* to include the physical and mental dimensions. God is in all of it. Our conditioned thinking may be preventing us from seeing this; but as we become more conscious, we begin to see God in all things. We will see nothing that is *not* spiritual.

I often avoid using the term *God* because many of us have a great deal of conditioning connected with that word. We have many subconscious (or conscious) images, memories, and feelings evoked when we hear the word *God*. Not all of these recollections are positive or helpful for us.

With this practice we want to experience what is real; we want to experience what is true. We want to experience God directly rather than become enamored with words or concepts about God. As I often remind my students, "If you are hungry, then it may be helpful to read a menu—but your hunger will not be satisfied until you eat the meal itself!"

Listen to or download the audio meditation for this practice at *unitybooks.org/living*.

# 5. PRACTICE 3:
## UNLIMITED FORGIVENESS

### What Is This Practice?

The practices of Radical Self-Awareness and Deep Self-Acceptance are called *self-related* practices. These practices focus on your personal internal experiences; even if you are interacting with another person, your primary focus is on your own experience. But some of the practices do involve your relationship with others. Practices 4 (Universal Benevolence) and 5 (Compassionate Communication) are examples; the focus of these practices is on how you are relating to others.

The practice of Unlimited Forgiveness is both self- and other-related: It relates to forgiveness of self and to forgiveness of others as well. When I explore my judgment of another, I see there is a component of self-judgment present as well. When I explore guilt, I see anger at someone else is usually present as well. Forgiveness needs to be applied in both directions: inward toward myself and outward toward others.

Forgiveness can be seen as having two phases. The first phase involves a decision I must make. The second stage is a process of healing that seems to have a life of its own. Let's look at the first phase: Here forgiveness is seen as a choice to let go of all blame and condemnation—of myself or another. Forgiveness is giving up all my stories of how wrong or bad someone has been and about how they (or I) deserve to be chastised for what they did or did not do.

It has been said forgiveness is giving up all hope for a better past! Forgiveness is about accepting a past experience and leaving it in the past; we then no longer carry it with us in the present moment.

A familiar Zen story tells of two monks traveling across the countryside when they encountered a young woman standing on a riverbank, too afraid to attempt a crossing of the river. Knowing they were forbidden to touch a woman, the first monk simply walked across the river to the other side, without looking at the girl. The second monk spoke to the girl and offered to carry her across the river. She accepted, and he did. After crossing the river, he put her down and she went on her way. After the two monks journeyed in silence for about an hour, the first monk began to criticize his friend for breaking a monastic vow. After berating him for several minutes, the second monk stopped and looked at his accusatory companion and said, "My friend, I put the girl down at the river's edge, but *you* have been carrying her for the past hour!"

In any moment we can choose to forgive or we can choose to condemn. We can choose to let go of our judgments or to hold on to them. If we choose to let our judgments go, they may return again a short time later. But in any given moment, we can choose, once again, to say, "I forgive you." We may need to do this again and again, particularly if our issue involves an offense that seems particularly egregious to us.

To understand the second phase of forgiveness as a process of healing, we must first look at the nature of unforgiveness. Unforgiveness is a mental stance in which we blame, condemn, and see someone as bad and wrong. Unforgiveness carries the desire for revenge; we want the offender to be rebuked or punished in some way.

Let's explore the experience of unforgiveness. If I am hurt physically or emotionally, I will feel pain, and sometimes feel it very intensely. If I am unwilling or unable to consciously experience this pain, then I will find a way to resist feeling it. A very common, almost instinctive way is to seek vengeance against the perpetrator. "An eye for an eye, a tooth for a tooth" is a very old way of assuaging our pain through some cathartic retribution.

As long as I focus on the evil nature of the offender, I do not have to feel the full impact of the pain I am experiencing. I attempt to stay focused on past events rather than on my own present moment experience. This response can be supported and reinforced by our cultural standards of good and bad, right and wrong.

Certainly there are some behaviors, such as murder, rape, or child abuse, which virtually everyone would agree are bad. I may feel totally justified in my blame and condemnation of the perpetrators of these acts. I can find a great deal of social support for this, but the price I pay for holding on to condemnation is a continuation of my own unhealed wounds, as well as a lack of self-awareness and perpetuation of my suffering.

To stop condemning the perpetrators does not mean I condone their actions. It simply means I no longer carry condemnation inside of me; I give up my demand that the past be different than it was. Forgiveness is the acceptance of what is and what was, putting the past in the past.

This same principle applies to guilt and self-blame as well. Even though guilt isn't any fun, it may actually be a defense against feeling some underlying pain. Like blame, guilt can become habituated; it can become part of one's identity.

To choose forgiveness means I must be willing to face and feel my pain in the present moment. This pain may have been created by the current event or it may be buried pain from the past simply resurrected by that event. Feeling our pain is never easy, but it is the beginning of the healing process. Feeling it is essential for the healing to occur.

The forgiveness process is similar to the grieving process: We go through stages. Anger is one of the stages of the grieving process, but anger does not need to turn into blame. If I engage anger with awareness and acceptance per our practices, then I am engaging in the forgiveness process. The key here is to focus on our own experience in the present moment—not on the past and not on the sins of another.

Forgiveness may involve feeling some underlying hurt or sadness; this is often part of the healing process. Forgiveness means feeling all your feelings for as long as they are present, and doing this without creating a story of martyrdom, victimhood, or self-righteousness. Just feel it directly without adding anything to it.

Feelings rarely make sense; they are not logical, and it is not their nature to be logical. Our life experiences may unearth some deeply buried pain, perhaps originating in the dim past. For example, someone criticizes something I have created. This person may have no malicious intent; maybe he is even trying to help me. But it could remind me of some buried and long-forgotten pain originating from criticism by my parents or teachers many years ago. It's important I don't dismiss this feeling just because it "doesn't make sense." It's even more important I don't make the other person the enemy and seek some form of revenge!

As you engage the forgiveness process, you may find blame keeps returning. This does not necessarily mean you have regressed; there can be many reasons why this happens. It's very common in the grieving process to temporarily revert to a prior stage. What to do when this happens? Simply choose to forgive once again.

The Gospel of Matthew (18:21-22 NRSV) contains a story of Peter asking Jesus, "Lord, if another member of the church sins against me, how often should I forgive? As many as seven times?" Jesus said to him, "Not seven times, but, I tell you, seventy-seven times." This essentially means "an unlimited

---

number of times," or the practice of Unlimited Forgiveness. We cannot put limitations on our forgiveness; otherwise it is not true forgiveness.

After many years of teaching and counseling, I have identified the following seven steps in the forgiveness process:

**1. See the Need for Forgiveness**

As you practice self-awareness and self-acceptance, recognize some of the symptoms of unforgiveness: desire for revenge; harsh criticism; avoidance or rejection of another person; a feeling that someone is "bad" or "wrong"; joy at someone else's difficulties. (Remember to apply this to self as well.)

**2. Be Willing to Forgive**

Forgiveness begins with a choice. See that forgiveness is about me; it is not about the other person. I may not be able to forgive completely right now, but I can be willing to begin the process. (However, it must come from choice, not from any sense of moral or spiritual obligation.)

**3. Ask for Help From Your Higher Power**

The ego does not want to forgive; it wants to hold on to the story, so we call upon our Higher Power, the God of our understanding. Perhaps this is what Jesus did as he was being nailed to the cross, when he said, "Father, forgive them; for they know not what they do" (Lk. 23:34). This is a good prayer to remember when we encounter circumstances or events beyond our personal power to understand.

**4. Give Up Condemnation**

This is the key. By being willing to give up condemnation, we begin the process of forgiveness. We may have to face an internal lobbyist who tries to convince us we should never let go of our resentment! This is simply a part of the ego defense system attempting to protect us from feeling the pain hidden by our condemnation. Remember, we choose forgiveness for our own healing. It does not matter whether or not the other person (or myself) "deserves" to be forgiven.

## 5. Face and Feel the Underlying Pain

This is typically the most difficult step. Very often the event that triggered our pain is not the real cause of it. Don't judge the intensity of your emotions by the nature of the triggering event. The triggering event may simply be the catalyst that fires up some dormant pain. Feelings will rarely make sense to the rational mind.

It can be very helpful to have a skillful method and a support system to help you work with strong emotions. Examples of a skillful method might be journaling, physical exercise, or being in nature. Learn to nurture yourself and to protect yourself when you feel raw or vulnerable. Examples of a support system might be confiding in a trusted friend, a counselor, or a recovery group. Spiritually based teachings may be especially helpful at these times.

## 6. Know the Truth

This is where you turn to your highest truth, whatever that may be, and however you may do that. Prayer, meditation, affirmations, chanting, sacred reading, and journal writing are some examples of ways to access your highest truth.

You may not be able to completely feel the truth you believe in, but that's not a problem. Just know there is a greater reality than your present experience may be presenting to you. It can be very helpful to have spiritual friends, teachers, and teachings available to help your remember at those times when it is easy to forget.

## 7. Repeat Steps 2-6 as Often as Necessary

Remember the teaching of "seventy-seven times." Be patient with yourself; the more intense the pain, the deeper the healing. And the deeper the healing, the more time it may take.

---

## What Forgiveness Is Not

True forgiveness has no limitations, no conditions, and no strings attached. It does not depend upon whether or not forgiveness is "deserved" or whether the perpetrators show remorse for what happened or even what their intent may have been. It is not a favor or blessing we bestow upon another; it is a blessing we bestow upon ourselves.

Our unforgiveness often stems from our own lack of understanding. We are very aware of our "side of the story" but often have little awareness of what is taking place in the life of another. Many of us have had the experience of judging someone, perhaps very harshly, and then upon hearing of the circumstances of this person's life, we found it very easy to forgive. When we can understand their situation, we may be able to feel some compassion for them.

A friend of Buddhist teacher Jack Kornfield told him the following story.

> In a hurry, I stood in line at the grocery store, impatiently waiting for the people in front of me. When it was almost my turn, I noticed the older woman in front of me engaged in an extended conversation with the young woman behind the checkout counter. This lady was holding a baby and the checker seemed to be very enamored by the baby and spent an inordinate amount of time smiling and talking to the child. I found myself becoming quite angry and judgmental. I said to myself, "This woman ought to be fired!" I considered reporting the incident to the store manager.
>
> Finally, just before the woman in front of me was about to depart, she turned to me and said, "I am sorry to keep you waiting. My daughter's husband died

unexpectedly and she has to work two jobs to make ends meet, and this is the only way that she is able to see her baby."[15]

Forgiveness may come easy in circumstances like this, but most of the time we will never know why people behave as they do; and we don't need to in order to forgive. Forgiveness always begins with a choice to forgive—whether we understand their behavior or not.

We are not bad if we are unable to forgive; perhaps we are just not ready. Sometimes the pain is so great we need to defend against it any way we can. A friend told me the story of a woman who was informed by her repentant husband that he had an affair with another woman. Her response was, "Someday I will forgive you, but right now I need to be outraged!"

When we are able to forgive, it does not make us morally superior, or a "better person." But it will make us a much happier person. Forgiveness is always its own reward.

## Why This Practice Is Transformative

In Jesus' teachings, as recorded in the Gospels, we see a consistent theme of how God's forgiveness of us is contingent upon our forgiveness of others. Some examples:

- For if you forgive others their trespasses, your heavenly Father will also forgive you; but if you do not forgive others, neither will your Father forgive your trespasses (Mt. 6:14-15 NRSV).
- Whenever you stand praying, forgive, if you have anything against anyone; so that your Father in heaven may also forgive you your trespasses (Mk. 11:25-26 NRSV).
- Do not judge, and you will not be judged; do not condemn, and you will not be condemned. Forgive, and you will be forgiven (Lk. 6:37 NRSV).

Many more related teachings are recorded in the Gospels. Although these accounts are written in mythic language that depicts a human-like God whose forgiveness is conditional, it points to an important universal principle. If we consider the "heavenly Father" as the archetype of wholeness that is evolving the universe into ever-greater awareness, freedom, and harmony, and is latent within each of us, then it may be easier to understand this profound teaching.

Our "heavenly Father" cannot forgive us because our own unforgiveness is prohibiting us from expressing the archetype of wholeness. My unforgiveness, regardless of my sense of justification, cuts me off from the source of my own wholeness. If I hold my breath and then pray for air, my prayer cannot be answered until I stop holding my breath and allow air into my lungs. God isn't punishing me for holding my breath, nor is he withholding the answer to my prayers. God cannot do anything for me when I refuse to accept the very thing I am asking for.

Unforgiveness is our refusal to acknowledge the principle of wholeness at work in our life. When I condemn anything or anyone, for any reason, I am restricting the experience of wholeness in my life. This is true even if I am not conscious of how or why I am restricting it.

Much of our unforgiveness is buried in the subconscious. As we practice Radical Self-Awareness and unconditional self-acceptance and cultivate the intention to forgive, we will discover any hidden experiences of unforgiveness. These blockages obscure our conscious experience of superconsciousness, which will restore our wholeness. Forgiveness is the process of returning to wholeness.

Whether we know it or not, we pay a huge price for our unforgiveness. Yes, the ego may feel gratified in being "right," but in reality that is very little compensation for the cost of it. This may be doubly true when the unforgiveness is directed toward oneself. Guilt, shame, and self-condemnation are particularly pernicious because, in a sense, we are paying twice. We pay the price all condemnation exacts, but we pay again because we are the target of our own condemnation.

One aspect of condemnatory judgment is the desire for the perpetrator to pay dearly for his misdeeds. When the convicted perpetrator is seen to be oneself, we become the criminal, judge, and executioner all wrapped up into one. We may feel we deserve to suffer for what we did or didn't do. This is rarely deliberate, or even conscious; much of the guilt we experience is the result of our past conditioning, which may not even be in alignment with our present conscious beliefs. Our old conditioning can run very deep. In the early 1960s, after the Second Vatican Council lifted the ban on eating meat on Friday, I (who was then Catholic) still felt guilty for eating meat on Friday for quite some time! Several friends shared similar experiences.

Forgiveness is an essential part of transformation, and self-forgiveness is especially important. Be patient with yourself, the roots of the unforgiveness may be very deep; but the ensuing freedom makes the work worthwhile many times over.

I will close this segment with a story from a wonderful movie titled *The Mission,* which was released in 1986. The story is set in the 1750s and involves Spanish Jesuit priest Father Gabriel (Jeremy Irons), who enters the South American jungle to build a mission and convert the native Guaraní community to Christianity. The Guaraní live above the perilous Iguazu Falls; it takes great effort to find them. After finding the Guaraní, Gabriel discovers a nearby Spanish settlement and encounters a mercenary and slaver named Rodrigo Mendoza (Robert De Niro) who makes his living kidnapping the Guaraní tribesmen and selling them to nearby plantations—including the plantation of the Spanish Governor.

One day Mendoza discovers his fiancée and his younger brother, Felipe, in bed together. He challenges Felipe to a duel, and kills him. Although acquitted of the killing by the Spanish Governor, Mendoza spirals into depression and guilt. Father Gabriel visits him and challenges Mendoza to undertake a suitable penance to expiate his guilt. Mendoza chooses his penance and accompanies the Jesuits on their return journey above the falls. His self-chosen penance is to pull a large bundle of heavy metal objects over and over again up the steep cliffs at the side of the falls. He would do this until he felt free from his guilt.

After pulling the load up the mountain many, many times, he still did not feel forgiven. One time, as he crawled to the top of the steep cliff, ropes and metal dangling from his exhausted body, he encountered a Guarani tribesman sitting there waiting for him. Mendoza is certain he will be killed because of his many crimes against this man's people. The tribesman grabs a machete and with a scowl, raises it high over his head. Knowing death is imminent, Mendoza lowers his head in anticipation of the fatal strike from the machete … and it comes down with a heavy whack!

The next scene shows the large bundle of metal objects rolling down the side of the cliff … the tribesman cut, not his neck, but the rope that bound him to all these heavy objects. Mendoza looks up in utter disbelief and begins to sob. Seeing his tears, the Guarani tribesman breaks into a contagious laughter that echoes throughout the forest. Soon even Mendoza's face is transformed by the laughter—and by the power of forgiveness.

### Forms of the Practice

As with previous practices, the basic forms are the general and the formal practice. The general practice is engaging the practice in your everyday life; formal practice is setting aside time specifically for the practice.

## General Practice

With the general practice, just live your life as normal; don't try to change your thoughts or your behavior. However, be attentive to any symptom of unforgiveness—however trivial it may seem. Instead of dismissing or rationalizing it away, use the experience to do this practice. Never miss an opportunity to practice forgiveness!

It's essential you employ Radical Self-Awareness and Deep Self-Acceptance as part of the forgiveness practice. Become especially aware of any symptom of unforgiveness, such as a negative judgment, criticism, gossip, or a sense of wanting to "get even." Also, notice any impatience, disappointment, or irritation.

In this practice, don't observe yourself like a traffic cop sitting at a speed trap. You are not trying to "catch yourself" in some kind of crime or sin. Practice awareness and acceptance, and notice the symptoms of unforgiveness if and when they arise; notice them without self-judgment or harshness. If self-judgment does arise, just see this as another opportunity to do the forgiveness work!

As you notice each experience of unforgiveness, you may begin to see a pattern emerge. You may see the same conditions seem to trigger the same feelings over and over again. For example, you might see that most of the time when you feel anger or judgment, it is because you feel rejected, put down, or discounted. This is an important awareness because it can point to an unrecognized wound and the conditions surrounding its origin. Yet it's important to not become overly analytical; just be aware without trying to analyze or interpret what shows up; deep insights usually arise spontaneously, without our analysis.

Please remember this practice refers to forgiveness of self as well as others. Sometimes this can be most difficult. Self-criticism is deeply embedded in the modern psyche; it can be very subtle—and few of us are totally free of it. Watch for any tendency to judge yourself for not doing the practices correctly. Sometimes we can unwittingly use the medicine to perpetuate the illness!

## Formal Practice

The formal practice can take many forms. One form is to sit for 10 minutes in the evening to review your day and become aware of any unforgiveness that may have occurred. Mentally review your day and notice any experiences of upset, disappointment, or conflict, however minor. At first you may not see very much at all, but as you continue the practice, you will become more attuned to even the most subtle experiences of unforgiveness.

Journal writing can be very helpful. Do it periodically, on a regular basis. Give yourself plenty of time for the process—at least 20 minutes, and more if possible. Keeping a journal and reviewing your entries over a period of time can help you to see any patterns present in the emotional responses to your life experiences.

Guided imagery meditation can also be very helpful. This can be self-led or led by another person or by a recording. One practice I have found helpful is to imagine you are standing before a very large house. See this as the house of your past, which contains many rooms on each floor. Imagine in each room there are individuals with whom you need to reconcile to make peace with your past. In your imagination, visit each of these rooms to see who is inside and hear what they have to say to you. If any conflict or pain arises, see if you can come to peace with that person or situation. If you cannot, then you can always revisit that room at another time. Be patient. This guided imagery can also be done as a journal writing process.

Most important, keep cultivating the intention to forgive. This intention will then be the force that guides you to whatever means may be helpful for you to engage the practice. Be patient with yourself.

## Perils on the Path

In general, the greatest peril for these practices is that the egoic patterns may try to co-opt the spiritual practice to reinforce the ego-pattern itself. I can unwittingly use my spiritual practice to reinforce the ego's story of being defective or incompetent or inherently unlovable. When I see how much (and how often) I judge myself and others, I can easily slide into a story of how "bad" or "defective" I am. When I find it is very difficult to forgive someone, I can fall into a story of being "incompetent" or "impotent" or "victimized" by my life circumstances.

It is very helpful if you are aware of these habituated tendencies so you can be alert to when you slip into these familiar stories; and when you do, to just let them go without adding more stories on top of them. It is also very helpful to remind yourself this is not a task to be accomplished; it is a spiritual discipline to be practiced, with clear intention and without attachment to results. Discouragement and self-judgment are not necessary or helpful in this practice; but if these arise, then just notice, accept, and forgive … again and again.

Another potential trap is to slip into facile or superficial forgiveness rather than true forgiveness. I may rationalize as a subtle way of denying my true feelings. This can be a way of bypassing the sometimes difficult work of real forgiveness. For example, if I am feeling critical of someone, I might rationalize it away by saying, "I shouldn't get so upset over something this trivial; it isn't too important." Doing this may seem to protect me from fully feeling the pain that underlies the judgment, but it deprives me of experiencing the healing that is an outcome of the forgiveness process.

Yet it is also important that we do not become identified with our sinfulness and psychically parade around in "sackcloth and ashes." This is what Mendoza unwittingly did in the *Mission* story. The Guarani tribesman who freed him may be symbolic of our own natural innocence that knows no guilt or shame. We are healed by the recognition of our own "Original Innocence."

## FAQ

**1.  You talk about judgment in a negative way, but isn't judgment necessary to function in the world?**

The word "judgment" has multiple meanings. In this chapter I usually refer to condemnatory judgment, wherein I judge someone as bad or sinful and deserving of some form of punishment. The word "judgment" can also mean *discernment*, which is indeed necessary and helpful to function in the world.

**2.  Are you saying  I should never be angry? Isn't it healthy to feel our anger?**

I am not saying we should ignore or suppress feelings of anger. Anger is a natural human emotion, but anger is not necessarily the same as condemnatory judgment, which is seeing someone as bad or defective or deserving to be punished. When I truly accept an emotional experience, I am acknowledging it is my personal experience. No one else is responsible for it; I don't need a story of "good guys and bad guys" to justify what I am feeling. Experiencing my feelings in a responsible way can be the first step toward forgiveness.

If I do find myself experiencing blame or condemnatory judgment toward anyone, I don't want to deny that either. If it is there, I want to see that it is there. But condemnation itself is a condition of nonacceptance. Forgiveness is accepting what is or was without adding a story onto it. Experiencing my natural feelings is not the same as holding on to a story of blame and condemnation.

**3. Is forgiveness always a good thing? What about criminals and terrorists—shouldn't they be punished for their crimes and atrocities?**

Yes, forgiveness is always a good thing; but forgiveness does not mean we never hold someone accountable for their actions. If someone steals from me, I can forgive them completely and still seek restitution. Criminals and terrorists may need to be incarcerated to protect the public from danger. Forgiveness is an internal experience; it does not necessarily mean we absolve someone of responsibility for their actions.

**4. Why is it so difficult to forgive myself?**

This is a very common question; there may be many reasons. Our culture encourages the quest for self-perfection. This may sometimes be motivated by an underlying feeling of being "not okay." Our contemporary emphasis on self-responsibility can easily slip into self-blame when something in our life seems to go wrong. We may hold higher expectations for ourselves than we do for others simply because we are typically more impacted by our own imperfections than by those of others.

Listen to or download the audio meditation for this practice at *unitybooks.org/living*.

# 6. PRACTICE 4:
# UNIVERSAL BENEVOLENCE

## What Is This Practice?

*Benevolence* is derived from a Latin word which means "a disposition of goodwill and kindness." *Universal Benevolence* is extending this disposition to all persons, and ultimately, to all beings. We may find it fairly easy to feel benevolent toward friends and loved ones. Extending this to all beings can be more challenging.

This practice is not so much about feeling benevolent as it is cultivating the intention of benevolence. Even if we do not feel particularly benevolent, we can still hold the intention to speak and to act from benevolence. The intention of benevolence can be expressed in our words and actions, even if we are not feeling "warm and fuzzy."

In the simplest language, this practice is about keeping your heart open as often as possible. Keeping our heart open may be easy to do when we feel safe and comfortable, but when we feel threatened or we're in pain, there's a very strong tendency to close our heart and to go unconscious. When this happens, just recognize it and return to your intention to keep your heart open.

If you cannot do this, just notice it without judgment or self-criticism. You can then see the circumstances that trigger your heart's closing and perhaps bring awareness, acceptance, and forgiveness to yourself and to others. This can result in a deep healing of your own heart as well as healing your relationships with others.

The practice of Universal Benevolence consists of cultivating three specific intentions: Appreciation, Kindness, and Generos-

---

ity. Each of these intentions includes the preceding one. Kindness springs from an attitude of appreciation, and generosity springs from an attitude of kindness. Appreciation softens the heart; kindness opens the heart; and generosity gives expression to that open heart. There is a natural progression from cultivating the attitude to taking concrete action.

Let's begin with the intention of appreciation. The word *appreciation* can be defined as "the recognition of the quality and the value of people and things." Interestingly, an alternative meaning of *appreciation* is to "increase in value," such as when a house appreciates in value. To practice appreciation is to recognize the value someone or something has for us, and *recognition itself increases the value* for us and for them.

Children learn of their own value via the appreciation of others—especially their parents. Even as adults, our personal sense of value may increase as we are appreciated by others.

Perhaps more important is the fact that as we appreciate others, we increase the recognition of our own value. Each of us is of infinite worth simply because our intrinsic nature is an expression of the ever-present origin. However, as a result of our conditioning, we often have difficulty recognizing our own value.

One way to recognize your own value is to practice appreciating others. At the psychological level, we experience our personal value by receiving the appreciation of others. At the spiritual level, we experience our inherent value by *giving* appreciation to others. *That which is innate in us can best be discovered by expressing it to others.*

Appreciation leads us to kindness. *Kindness* is defined as "a friendly, warm-hearted, and empathetic nature." The word is derived from an Old English word that references the natural feeling of kindness a family has for its members. Typically, we find it easier to be kind to "our own kind." Through the practice of Universal Benevolence, we see that "our own kind" includes every living being.

While appreciation is primarily an internal practice, kindness is both an internal and an external practice. Kindness begins internally by cultivating a particular attitude, yet kindness can also be expressed in words and actions. There are no limits to the possible expressions of kindness.

Generosity is a natural outgrowth of kindness. Generosity may be defined as "the willingness to give liberally and to give often." A synonym for the word "generosity" is "magnanimity," which literally means "having a great soul." Indeed, the practice of generosity can "enlarge" our soul.

Generosity also has limitless avenues of expression. We can be generous with our possessions, with our time, with our talents, and with our attention. Generosity is expressed in our actions but it always begins with an attitude: the willingness to give at every opportunity. The practice of generosity, in turn, reinforces the capacity for appreciation in both the giver and the receiver. As Shakespeare tells us, "It is twice blest: It blesseth him that gives and him that takes."[16]

Although the practice of Universal Benevolence is generally practiced in relation to others, it is very important to extend appreciation, kindness, and generosity to oneself, in both attitude and deed. This might be mistakenly equated with egocentricity or self-indulgence, but they are not the same—they are very different. True benevolence is not conditional or based upon performance; nor does it seek to make us superior to anyone else. True benevolence both appreciates our uniqueness and unites us all as equals.

Universal Benevolence is a generic term I am using to identify the three interrelated practices of Appreciation, Kindness, and Generosity. In actual practice, these appear to be inseparable; they are simply three facets of the same gem of truth expressed by Jesus when he said, "This is my commandment, that you love one another as I have loved you" (Jn. 15:12).

The practice of Universal Benevolence is being willing to extend this love unconditionally to all persons, and ultimately, to all beings. Extending this to all beings can sometimes be very challenging, especially if some of those beings have caused us a great deal of suffering. But true benevolence is universal; it has no exceptions.

Pol Pot became leader of Cambodia in April, 1975. Throughout the next 20 years, more than 2 million Cambodians (25 percent of the total population) died in his regime's infamous killing fields. Maha Ghosananda, a respected Cambodian monk, would often go into refugee camps where thousands of people had fled the terrible holocaust. Every family there had lost children, spouses, and parents to the ravages of genocide, and their homes and temples had been destroyed. On one occasion, Maha Ghosananda announced to the refugees there would be a Buddhist ceremony the next day, and all who wished to come would be welcome. Since Buddhism had been savagely desecrated by Pol Pot, many people were curious if anyone would dare to show up.

The next day, more than 10,000 refugees converged at the meeting place to share in the ceremony. It was an enormous gathering. Maha Ghosananda sat for some time in silence on a platform in front of the crowd. Some wondered what he would say. What could one possibly say to this group of people who had lost so much? What he did next, in the company of these refugees, was begin to repeat a verse from the Dhammapada, a sacred Buddhist scripture.

> Hatred never ceases by hatred; but by love alone is healed.
> This is an ancient and eternal law.

These were people who had as much cause to hate as anyone on earth. Yet as Maha Ghosananda sat there, chanting this verse over and over, one by one, thousands of voices joined together in unison: "Hatred never ceases by hatred: but by love alone is healed. This is an ancient and eternal law." People started weeping. They had been through so much sorrow, so much pain; just to hear the sound of these words was precious.

Out of the mouths of people who had been wounded, oppressed, made homeless, aggrieved, and crushed by the pain of war, came a prayer proclaiming the ancient truth about love; a truth that was greater than all the sorrows they had seen and felt: "Hatred never ceases by hatred: but by love alone is healed. This is an ancient and eternal law."[17]

### Why This Practice Is Transformative

Transformative spiritual practice is a discipline we engage to liberate us from bondage to an illusory ego-identity. Transformative practice disrupts the ego's habituated patterns of unconsciousness. As we become disengaged from the ego-identity, we obtain glimpses of the ever-present origin. Spiritual practice then supports our experience of the origin as it emerges. As we experience our original nature, our identity begins to shift from the false to the real: We come home to that which we truly are. Spiritual practice is the ultimate act of self-love.

The ego's inclination is always in the direction of its own self-interest. It's always thinking, "What about me ... me ... me?" and is continuously afraid of not getting what it believes it needs to survive. The ego is preoccupied with getting what it wants and of avoiding what it doesn't want. When identified with ego, we are constantly trying to prove we are right, we are good, and we are in control. As children, when the ego structure is developing, these desires may be appropriate, but if we continue this pattern as adults, we can create chaos and suffering for ourselves and for others.

It's important to have a healthy ego so we can function effectively. If there is a developmental deficiency in the ego-structure, it may be helpful to engage in psychotherapy or some other healing modality. Just as we need a healthy body to function in the world, we need a healthy ego as well. The ego, as well as the body, is an important part of our human identity; but we are more than the body, and we are more than the ego. Spiritual practice takes us beyond identification with either of these.

The practice of Universal Benevolence moves us beyond egocentricity. We don't neglect ourselves, but the primary focus is not on oneself—it is on others. The practice of appreciation emphasizes the value and the positive qualities of others. The intention of kindness focuses on the needs of others as much as our own. Generosity transforms the ego's tendency for acquisition to that of sharing and giving. Universal Benevolence expands the desire for happiness beyond oneself to include all beings.

Transformative practice mirrors the natural state of a spiritually awakened individual. Someone who is fully awake to the ever-present origin will naturally express Universal Benevolence. To this person, it is not a spiritual practice; it is just a natural state of being. An awakened person behaves this way simply because she knows the truth and lives in reality.

Transformative practice will bring the ego's hidden attachments and resistances into conscious awareness. Without such a practice, these tendencies can go unnoticed for many years but with a huge price in terms of personal dissatisfaction and interpersonal conflict. When we experience this resistance as it arises, it does not mean we have made a mistake or we aren't doing the practice correctly. On the contrary, the more we engage the practice, the more likely these previously hidden obstacles will arise.

Simply recognizing resistance without reacting to it is a major part of the transformative process. Another big part is being willing to consciously experience whatever is beneath the resistance. Below our resistance lies an unhealed wound, and with it, a certain amount of unfelt pain. The wound is unhealed because it has not been recognized and experienced consciously. The healing lies in seeing and feeling this pain without suppressing it, acting it out, or engaging in drama. We just see it, accept it, feel it, and let it go.

We see, in the long run, there is far less suffering in facing and feeling our pain than there is in continued resistance to it. Denying our present discomfort usually leads to greater long-term suffering. When a wound remains hidden and unhealed, it functions as an invisible attractor that influences our behavior and shapes our life experiences. It can be like the gravitational force that affects all life on earth: invisible, yet very powerful. To ignore it is unwise.

We may also find resistance may arise in the form of another person or in a life condition or circumstance. Sometimes we are not aware of any internal resistance, but we can be painfully aware of some external resistance. I recall a woman once approaching me in great confusion. She said, "Ever since I asked God to make me a more loving person, all these terrible people have come into my life! What's wrong?" I did my best to explain to her that perhaps nothing was wrong, and maybe her prayer was being answered, although she was not seeing it that way.

Whether the resistance seems to be coming from within you or from something external, it ultimately doesn't matter. Simply continue the practice of Universal Benevolence, which includes the previous practices of self-awareness, self-acceptance, and forgiveness.

As we persist in the practice, we will eventually discover our original nature hidden beneath the resistance that initially pre-occupied our attention. The power of our original nature gradually becomes the new attractor, much stronger than the gravity of the ego. The qualities of Universal Benevolence increasingly become natural to us.

You will also begin to discover the joy of benevolence. This is not the ego's short-lived pride of accomplishment, but rather a genuine quality of joy arising from the wellspring of your own original nature. And, your joy increases as you share it with others!

## Forms of the Practice

We begin by looking at our formal practice periods. Here we focus on each subpractice separately for a period of time and then integrate it into the general practice. Ideally, each formal practice period is about 20 minutes per day. We work with appreciation for a week or so and then move on to kindness practice for a similar period, and finally, to the generosity practice, gradually incorporating all three of these into daily life. And remember, each practice automatically includes the preceding practice.

As you engage these practices, remember this is primarily a process of cultivating intention: the intention of appreciation, kindness, and generosity. Don't see this as a goal to be achieved but rather a practice in which to engage; some days you will do it well and some days you may forget. Yes, we do want to actively express these in everyday life, but it all begins with intention. The formal practice will serve to strengthen your intention to bring the practice into daily life. There are no standards of perfection; just do the practice as best you can. The only way to do it wrong is to not do it at all! Always remember to include yourself in the practices.

## Appreciation

1. Think about what you value. Consider who and what in your life is important to you. Make a list; be as specific as possible.
2. For each person and item you listed, identify specifically what it is you appreciate. For example, if you listed your spouse, then what is it about him or her that evokes appreciation in you? If you listed your work, then what is it about your work you appreciate?
3. Choose some of the people from your list and write them a letter that begins: "Thank you for being in my life ..." (You may give them this letter, but it is not necessary to do so.)
4. Do the same for people who may no longer be in your life, but with whom you value having spent time. Once again, be as specific as possible.
5. Do the same for yourself; be specific about what you appreciate about yourself. Write yourself a letter. Keep it, and refer to it many times in the future.
6. Meditate each day with gratitude for the innate goodness of life in its variety of forms.

## Kindness

1. Think of individuals you know. Imagine their face and bring them into your heart. Silently wish them well. Give them a blessing such as "May you be happy. May you be healthy. May you be prosperous."
2. Consider doing the same for people you hear about in the news who may be suffering from some tragedy such as catastrophic weather, earthquakes, wars, or shootings.
3. Do the same for yourself.
4. Meditate each day with an open heart of love that is pouring forth kindness to all living beings.

## Generosity

1. Building upon the previous practices, sit quietly and ask, "What can I give? To whom can I give? How can I give?" Write down the responses to your questions.
2. As you consider generosity practice, look at some of the potential obstacles that may arise for you in the form of fears, beliefs, or past conditioning. Write these down. How does it feel to examine them?
3. Meditate each day with an open heart of magnanimity. Visualize yourself as a vessel for universal abundance. How does that feel?

## General Practice

### Appreciation

Start each day with the intention to be aware of what has value for you and what you appreciate in your life. Throughout your day, be aware of who and what you appreciate and silently say, "Thank you!" When the opportunity presents itself, say this aloud to someone. And always be aware of new ways to appreciate yourself!

### Kindness

Start each day with the intention to be kind at every opportunity. Throughout your day, be open to opportunities to express kindness through word or action. Each time you meet someone, ask yourself, "How can I express kindness? How can I be truly helpful?" Look for opportunities to be genuinely kind to yourself.

### Generosity

Start each day with the willingness to give at every opportunity. Throughout the day, be open to opportunities to express generosity in some way. Each day look for new ways to give of your possessions, time, talents, and yourself. Become aware of the subtle ways you may avoid giving because of fear, resentment, or some old belief patterns.

## Perils on the Path

### The Far Enemies

The far enemy can take several forms, but the feeling tone is very similar in each. The far enemy of appreciation is contempt, scorn, or prejudice. The far enemy of kindness is cruelty, hatred, or indifference. And the far enemy of generosity is greediness, avarice, or acquisitiveness.

These far enemies have the potential to be very destructive, especially if we speak or act from these negative energies. They are problematic also because they serve to strengthen the ego. By diminishing another person, I am attempting to inflate my own ego. We can become very self-righteous in our condemnation of others!

If I am engaged in condemning another person, I need to take an honest look at myself and ask, "What am I refusing to see within myself? What pain of my own am I trying to avoid?" Be kind to yourself. Condemning yourself for condemning another will only compound the negativity!

### The Near Enemies

Pity is a near enemy of benevolence. Appreciation, kindness, and generosity are not the same as pity. We may feel compassion when another is suffering, but compassion is not pity. With pity, we see the other person as a victim, as someone diminished by their circumstances. And we may, as the benefactor, feel superior in relationship to the receiver; we may see ourselves as a rescuer or some type of hero. This is not true benevolence.

Benevolence is not the same as codependency. Codependency arises when we feel a deficiency within ourselves and then attempt to find our own value by pleasing others. Codependency can appear as love and kindness, but internally it's motivated by lack and fear. It is characterized by an inability to set appropriate personal boundaries.

Universal Benevolence does not negate the need to set appropriate boundaries; it integrates wisdom and discernment with love and kindness.

It's important to recognize our own limits and abilities to give or to serve.

To become burned out or taken advantage of is not a spiritual practice; lack of self-care is not benevolence or kindness to anyone.

Benevolence does not arise from a sense of deficiency or dependency. It is not an attempt to bolster a weak self-image, or to compensate for a feeling of deficiency. It does not attempt to impress others or to project a particular image. True benevolence is always a choice, not a compulsion.

Appreciation, kindness, and generosity arise naturally from the recognition that we are all expressions of the ever-present origin, and we are all interconnected in very intimate ways. With this awareness, benevolence is natural and joyful. We help others because they are a part of ourselves.

The practice of benevolence for all beings certainly includes oneself. It's when we fail to appreciate ourselves that we become addicted to getting our value from others. Universal Benevolence is a spiritual practice where we bestow kindness upon ourselves as readily as we do others.

### FAQ

**1. How can I possibly practice benevolence for the likes of Adolph Hitler or Osama bin Laden? And I can't imagine feeling benevolent toward a rapist or a child molester.**

The practice begins with the people in your own life, the persons with whom you come in contact day to day. Begin with the persons in your life and then widen the circle to the extent you are able. These practices are primarily about your personal life experience; don't worry too much about hypothetical "what-ifs."

Practicing benevolence toward someone does not mean you necessarily approve of their behavior or agree with their beliefs; it simply means you are willing to open your heart to all human beings who come into your life. If you cannot do it with someone, then simply continue the practice as best you can with all the others.

Remember, the purpose of the practice is our own transformation; we aren't doing it because someone else *deserves* our benevolence. We do it because it is our chosen spiritual practice. It has nothing to do with the merit, or lack of merit, in anyone else.

## 2. Isn't feeling benevolence toward oneself a form of egotism?

Not as it is prescribed in this practice. Feeling benevolence for myself doesn't mean I believe I am better than anyone else. It is not a form of pride in which I have earned my own benevolence because I'm smart or competent. Benevolence as described in this chapter is simply a genuine and unconditional caring for oneself and for others, with no strings attached. This is not egotism.

## 3. Can't this practice sometimes be a form of dishonesty? If I am angry with someone, trying to feel benevolence is inauthentic and denies my true feelings.

Remember, we are not necessarily trying to *feel* a certain way. Cultivate a general attitude of benevolence and act upon it as may be appropriate. If you are angry with someone, you may not be feeling particularly benevolent, but this doesn't need to negate your intention and willingness to practice benevolence in some form.

Benevolence doesn't mean you don't honestly communicate your feelings, but it *does* mean you communicate with as much kindness as possible. If you're angry with someone, first look at your own feelings, and at what lies beneath the feeling of anger, before speaking to the other person. You can speak to them *about* your anger without speaking *from* the anger. You *can* speak from your anger with the intention of kindness and without compromising honesty or authenticity. This may take some practice, and you may not do it perfectly every time. Just do your best, and be kind to yourself.

Listen to or download the audio meditation for this practice at *unitybooks.org/living*.

# 7. PRACTICE 5:
# COMPASSIONATE COMMUNICATION

We began the five foundational practices with Self-Aware-ness and then moved onto the cultivation of Self-Acceptance, Forgiveness, and Benevolence. We complete this foundation by integrating these into the practice of Compassionate Commu-nication.

It's in relationship with others that we find our greatest joys and our greatest challenges. In relationship with others, we most often fall into our unconscious patterns of thought and behavior. It's in relationship with others we often find the most difficulty sustaining our practice of Awareness and Benevo-lence. For these reasons, our relationships with others may offer us the greatest potential for transformation.

Many of our life experiences seem incomplete if we have not shared them with another person. Perhaps nothing impacts the quality of our life more than the quality of our relationships. And perhaps nothing impacts the quality of our relationships more than the quality of our communication.

## What Is This Practice?

Compassionate Communication* is a process that connects us deeply to our own internal experiences and to the deepest part of others. It has the potential to transform our relation-ships, our culture and, most important, ourselves. Compassion-ate Communication includes speaking and listening, reading

---

*Nonviolent Communication, a process developed by Marshall Rosenberg, is sometimes referred to as Compassionate Communication. I am not specifically referencing this when I use the term; I am using the term in a more general and inclusive way. The primary intention for the practice described in this book is not exactly the same as that of Rosenberg's NVC.

and writing. It incorporates our previous four practices. Intention and awareness are key factors in this practice.

It can be extraordinarily enriching when two or more persons have consciously engaged this practice with similar intentions, but it is *not* crucial. We can engage this practice in virtually any circumstance, whether others are practicing it or not. No one else even needs to know we are engaging the practice.

It is very important that we engage this practice with clear understanding and intention. The intention is *not* to change another person, or to get them to agree with you. It's not even to have them understand you. *The primary intention must be your own personal transformation* as you engage this practice. If this occurs, your relationships will inevitably improve, but this is a by-product, rather than a primary intention.

## Right Speech

The core of this practice lies in the Buddhist teaching of Right Speech. The term *Right* refers to "that which supports spiritual practice and leads to transformation." It is not a rule or a commandment that declares what is the right or proper speech to which we must rigidly adhere. The term "Right" does not imply there is only one right way; there are an infinite number of ways to practice Right Speech.

This teaching supports a transformative spiritual practice. We practice it as we would practice any new skill, such as playing a musical instrument or learning a new language. In this context, mistakes are not really mistakes because that is where our learning takes place. We can learn more from doing something wrong than from doing it right!

An important part of this practice is noticing when you are *not* practicing Right Speech. Become aware of your internal experience: your thoughts, emotions, and body sensations. If you find yourself violating the practice guidelines then you may be unconsciously resisting something that needs your attention. The practice guidelines are like the rumble strips on the edge of a highway that warn us when we are wandering off the road. This gives us the opportunity for deeper self-awareness and allows us to see into the relationship between our state of mind and the quality of our speech.

Here are guidelines for Right Speech: Before I speak (or write), I consider:

- Is it true?
- Is it kind?
- Is it necessary?

Before I communicate, I consider the question "Is it true?" I do not present anything as true I know is false or is questionable. If I say something I believe is true and discover later it's not true, then I do whatever I can to correct the error. This is my guide for Right Speech.

If I find myself saying something I know is not true, it's very important to explore the motive behind my action. Was I motivated by fear or anger? Was I trying to avoid some feeling? For example, if I tell my friend I like her new car when I really don't, I could dismiss this as simply being polite or nice. If I am really honest with myself, I might see I fear speaking honestly because I am afraid if I do, she may discontinue our friendship, or she will judge me as unkind or disloyal. I can then explore what's behind the fear ... perhaps a feeling of loneliness ... or of shame.

This then gives me an opportunity to see how I maintain all my relationships. Do I believe it's not safe to tell the truth? Do I believe I am responsible for someone else's feelings? Am I truly honest in my relationships or are they based upon some façade? If I am avoiding something, then I may see there's a piece of my personal history I am unwilling to embrace, therefore not allowing it to heal.

Sometimes I may want to share my particular point of view on a certain topic, such as a political issue. My intention might be to change someone else's point of view or at least to help them see the value of my perspective.

Can I do this without violating the tenets of Right Speech? The answer is, "Yes, but I must remember what I am saying is simply *my* point of view, and not speak as if I am conveying an absolute and eternal truth which they must accept."

I can speak my views and my opinions with passion and with zeal, but the key question is, "How attached am I to my point of view being the *only* right way to see this issue?" Right Speech rests upon intention: Am I seeking self-transformation or am I trying to change someone else?

Before I communicate, I consider the question, "Is it kind?" Kindness is not necessarily the same as being polite, nice, or politically correct; and kindness is not flattery. Kindness begins with the heart's intention. It begins with appreciation and genuine caring. There's nothing wrong with being polite or politically correct, but these are fairly superficial. True kindness is conveyed beyond the words themselves.

Kindness arises from the heart and cannot be contained in a formula or prescription. I am sometimes asked, "What happens if I must choose between kindness and honesty?" My response is, "I don't believe it has to be an 'either/or' decision; kindness and truth are not incompatible." Perhaps the relevant question is, "How do I speak the truth *and* be kind at the same time?" It may take some practice to develop this skill, but it is entirely possible to do so. I always need to be aware of my intention in the process.

A third guideline I apply: "Is it necessary to speak at all?"

I again look at my intention: "Is my speech motivated by an authentic desire to share with another?" "Am I speaking with concern for another's well-being? Or am I attempting to impress or influence another person?" "Am I trying to defend or justify myself in some way?" "Am I attached to a particular outcome?" "Am I aware of feeling any fear or anger before I speak?"

If I bring Radical Self-Awareness into my life activities, I begin to discover the intention behind what I do. Do I speak to convey information or to deepen relationships? Or do I speak to fortify my ego, to relieve anxiety, to impress someone, or to control a situation?

When we do this, it does not make us a bad person, but it does hinder our transformation. It keeps us unconscious by perpetuating habituated defenses. These patterns are counter-transformational and rob us of true intimacy and true self-expression.

The next time you are at a social gathering or any circumstance where folks are gathered to visit, notice your motivation to speak and see what arises if you don't indulge the impulse to talk. What's it like to simply "show up" and be present to yourself and to others without being obliged to speak? This can be a very revealing experience!

On the other hand, if you find it much easier to keep quiet and blend into the crowd, then the next time you have the desire to speak, see if you can act upon this desire. If you find that difficult, then what is it you fear? What is the internal "censor" saying to you? What might you feel when you just speak from the heart rather than rehearse or censor your words? Right Speech means applying intention, not censorship to our speech.

**Listening**

Speech alone does not comprise communication; there must be listening. Compassionate listening is as important as compassionate speech. Let's explore this.

We begin by distinguishing between hearing and listening. If you speak to me in a language I do not understand, then I may be hearing, but I cannot truly listen; there is no communication. If you speak to me, but I'm preoccupied with something else, then my ears may hear your words, but there is no true listening—and no communication.

Listening occurs in degrees. I can hear the same words from four different speakers, but my listening may be very different with each of them.

The speaker may be skillful and clear, but the listener may not be! Let's explore four different levels of listening, which results in four different levels of communication.

The lowest level of listening is when I hear the words of another person, but I am totally preoccupied with my own thoughts and judgments. I am listening more intently to my own internal conversation, and I am more preoccupied with how I will express my own views on the topic than I am with anything you are saying. A classic example of this is the "debates" between politicians in an election year. Their intention is to listen to the other person only to the extent they can prove him wrong and show they have a much better idea. Their real intention is to communicate with the TV audience rather than their opponent. This level of communication is not limited to politicians; it can be found in homes and offices everywhere!

The next level of listening occurs when I am more open to what the speaker has to say, and I may even enjoy what she is saying, but everything I hear is received only at the level of my intellect. There may be some willingness to learn, but little desire on my part to be deeply touched or to be changed. I listen politely and respond with interest and without animosity or disagreement, but I am not really changed as a result of this interaction. This level of hearing is probably the norm for our culture. Its primary intention is to maintain and reinforce the existing ego structure of the listener and perhaps the speaker as well. It is usually a large part of the unspoken agreement surrounding our polite social interactions.

The third level of listening is when I am honestly willing to be changed as a result of my interaction with the other person. I am willing to keep my heart open and to understand the speaker in a deep way. I am willing to enter into a true dialogue with the other person so we are both deepened and enriched as an outcome. This type of listening is necessary for psychotherapy, spiritual direction, and life coaching. It is vitally important for truly intimate relationships.

The fourth level of listening transcends our usual concept of "listening." Here, both the speaker and the listener enter into a field of listening to Spirit as it speaks to both of us. We enter with a complete openness of mind, heart, and soul. It is the basis of what philosopher Martin Buber called an "I-Thou" relationship. I must enter into this relationship with what Zen Buddhists call Beginner's Mind: the mind that opens to each experience as if for the very first time, with no prejudices and no agenda. This experience is sometimes called "Presencing." This type of communication is rare and precious and is what most of us deeply desire.

This level of communication is therapeutic in the deepest meaning of the term *therapy*, which means "to heal." It is true intimacy, it is deeply healing, and it can be very difficult. It's difficult because I must be open to every facet of myself and the other. I must be willing to be changed at depth. I must be willing to face my greatest fear and to feel both the deepest pain and the utmost joy imaginable. It is the epitome of vulnerability; and it is one of the most sublime experiences one can have as a human being.

Compassionate Communication requires us to be willing to go beyond our comfort zone and beyond ourselves (as we know ourselves to be). It requires Radical Self-Awareness and Deep

Self-Acceptance; it requires the willingness to forgive without limitation and to open our heart to anyone and everyone.

To avoid misunderstanding, I want to make two important points. First, I want to distinguish between vulnerability and gullibility. Vulnerability does not negate discernment, which is part of our essential nature.

Vulnerability requires giving up defensiveness; but defensiveness is not the same as discernment. To be totally open and vulnerable to another person does not require that I surrender my will to that person. I surrender my will to my own essential nature, but not to another human being. Not understanding this distinction has caused a great deal of suffering in many spiritual communities.

Second, these levels of listening are descriptive, not prescriptive. There is no "Thou shalt ..." to any of these. I do not put a value judgment or moral evaluation on any of the levels; none of them are universally right or wrong. The important questions are, "What do I really want?" "Am I willing to open and be deeply changed to get what I really want?" If I desire transformation, I must be open to being changed at depth. But, if transformation is not what I want right now, then that is perfectly okay as well. Transformation never occurs through coercion, whether it's self-generated or external.

### Why This Practice Is Transformative

Our relationships act as mirrors that reflect unseen parts of our self. Our hidden wounds, as well as our latent talents and concealed strengths, can be revealed in our relationships with others. Our greatest joy and our deepest suffering most often occur in relationship to others.

Many spiritual traditions, in both the East and the West, rely upon intentional community as part of their practice. Christian monasteries, Buddhist sanghas, Sufi communities, and other spiritual communities are formed to create a vessel that will both support and challenge the individual yogi* in his or her path of awakening. How we experience the relationships in our life forms an essential part of the spiritual journey.

The most important relationship we have is the one with our own true nature. This relationship deeply influences all the others. A spiritual community encourages each member to cultivate this relationship as the basis for all others. Some form of conscious communication with one's essential self, as well as with others, is the intention of each spiritual aspirant in the community.

We are deeply conditioned by our early relationships with family, peer group, and culture. How we interact with others reflects this personal and cultural conditioning. *How we relate to our own essential nature is impacted by this conditioning as well.* This conditioning is largely invisible; it is like the ocean is to a fish: It is ubiquitous, but invisible. By becoming aware of how we communicate (or fail to communicate) as we do, we begin to see into the deeper layers of this conditioning. As we become free from our conditioning, our relationship to our essential self, as well as our relationship to others, is transformed.

As we communicate more consciously and compassionately with others, we will also communicate more consciously and compassionately with each aspect of our self. Love is not directional; it always flows inward and outward simultaneously. Transforming our self and transforming our relationships are simply two dimensions of the same process. Compassion is the key: Compassion for self, as well as for others. Compassionate Communication is love in expression.

---

*This word *yoga* means *union* in Sanskrit. I use the term *yogi* to mean any individual engaged in a spiritual practice aimed at union with the divine.

## Forms of the Practice

As we do with the other practices, we have both general and formal forms of this practice. The primary practice is the general practice that occurs in our everyday life, yet it can be very helpful to engage in formal practice as well. Let's address each of these forms.

In the everyday life practice, we begin with the stated intentions of compassionate speech and compassionate listening. Pay attention to your speech and listening throughout the day and notice how your actual communication compares with your intentions. When you see a significant disparity between intention and actual behavior, explore what you were feeling as you acted as you did. The intention is not to figure out how to do it right, but rather to gain self-awareness, to learn something about yourself. Every apparent misstep is an opportunity to learn; and *this* is the primary intention. We seek to learn how we are unconsciously undermining awareness of our own essential nature.

Others do not need to know you are doing this practice, and it doesn't matter if others are communicating compassionately or not. In fact, we can often learn more when they are not, because that tends to trigger our own unconscious patterns. So ironically, it may work even better for us if others are *not* being skillful or compassionate in their communication! This doesn't make the practice easier, but it can make it more productive.

There are several types of formal practice. One form is to have a spiritual friend with whom you can share your experiences and give feedback throughout the day, or at the end of the day. If you live or work with this person, you may be able to do it on the spot as it is occurring; this can be extremely helpful. If not, you can still converse at the end of the day to share, support, and give feedback to one another.

You can also engage in this feedback process on your own via journal writing. At the end of each day, spend about 20 minutes writing about how you engaged (or did not engage) the practice throughout the day. Note the impact of skillful communication as well as the unskillful communication. Inquire into the experiences that were unskillful to explore thoughts and feelings that were active in you at those times. Be curious, yet always compassionate with yourself. It can be helpful to periodically review your journal.

Remember, the intention of the practice is to learn; it is not to get results or to do it perfectly. It *can* be very gratifying when you engage the practice skillfully and see the positive results that ensue; but this is a by-product—it is not the primary goal. This practice *will* transform your relationships, but the most important relationship of all is the one with your own essential self.

**Perils on the Path**

The far enemy of this practice is to communicate with violence, judgment, or lack of compassion. This could take the form of judgment, criticism, gossip, or belittlement. Or it may be more subtle, such as refusing to listen to another, or discounting their attempt to communicate with us. This can happen when we forget to include the other core practices and become unconscious.

The far enemy of every spiritual practice has unconsciousness at its core. When this occurs, it's very helpful to notice any patterns present in the circumstances surrounding our unconscious behavior. For example, I may tend to go unconscious when I am with others who are gossiping or complaining. I may feel a compelling need to join in with my own version of "ain't it awful." Or I may go into an unconscious pattern when I hear someone appear to criticize me; perhaps this triggers a story that I am incompetent, or it may resurrect memories of abuse I experienced in the past.

Perhaps a particular topic triggers an unconscious pattern of speech. Some of us have certain "hot buttons" that will send us into a tirade. A few years ago, I was at a meditation retreat with a group of individuals practicing various forms of self-awareness. The communication was quite civil and compassionate until we got onto the subject of politics; then everything changed! Many of the formerly compassionate and serene individuals seemed to quickly morph from Dr. Jekyll into Mr. Hyde.

It may be a particular person or event that trips me up and takes me into the black hole of unconsciousness. Whatever it is, it is very helpful to see any patterns that are present. To do this, it is important to be as objective and nonjudgmental of yourself as possible. Self-judgment just leads to further unconsciousness.

The near enemy of a spiritual practice masquerades as the practice itself, but is actually a subtle form of unconscious resistance. It can be the most "dangerous" enemy because it is often the most difficult to identify. One near enemy of this practice is to seemingly engage in Compassionate Communication but to do it with egocentric intentions. For example, I may appear to engage the practice very well, but I am doing so because I want others to like me, or I want to get them to see things my way. The practice is then used as a tool to fulfill the intentions of the ego.

Another enemy of most any practice is the presence of perfectionism or self-judgment. When we begin any awareness practice, one of the first things we usually see is just how *unaware* we can be! Likewise, we may feel chagrined at seeing how uncompassionate our speaking or listening can be. It's important to not become self-critical because this is quite normal. Perfectionism is one of the greatest enemies of transformation because it keeps you tied to an idealized image of self rather than allowing you to open up to what you really are.

Attachment to specific outcomes can lead to doubt and discouragement; and this may seduce you into abandoning the practice. If you are aware of feeling discouraged, look to see what expectations you may be holding. Intention is not the same as expectation; intention is setting a course in a specific direction and then returning to that intention every time you stray from it. We do not know our ultimate destination; it is an open-ended process of continuous unfoldment—there is no "finish line" to be crossed.

## FAQ

**1. This practice seems artificial. I feel like I can't speak authentically.**

Anytime we engage a new discipline, it may feel a bit strange at first because we are disrupting some deeply ingrained patterns. With this practice, you *can* be fully authentic in acknowledging your present experience—whatever it is—with another person, provided it is shared as *your own experience*.

Authenticity means we take responsibility for our own experience and then communicate it honestly. What we interrupt with this practice is not authenticity but the habituated patterns that keep us unconscious and may be harmful to others. Gossip, criticism, and blame may seem normal to some of us, but this is *not* authenticity.

This practice is about wedding authenticity with compassion. This takes some practice, but it is certainly possible and well worth the effort in terms of personal freedom and deeper intimacy in our relationships.

We practice primarily for personal transformation; however, you will see this work greatly improves your relationships with others.

---

## 2. How do I communicate compassionately to a person in my life who is very negative most of the time?

It's important to remember this practice does not depend on any particular response from another person; we are doing this for our own transformation. Also, remember this practice is predicated upon the previous practices.

Ask yourself: *What thoughts, emotions, and sensations do I experience as my friend speaks? Can I allow these feelings to be felt without suppression or self-judgment? Am I willing to be nonjudgmental? Am I willing to be benevolent?*

If the answer is "yes" to these questions, Compassionate Communication will feel more natural. Notice none of this requires us to agree with our friend or to support what he is saying. We might even share our disagreement with him if we can do so with awareness and compassion. If I do express my disagreement, then what is my intention? Am I attached to "correcting" my friend or defending my point of view?

When you see these circumstances as opportunities for your own transformation, they can become very rich opportunities for practice. If you are attached to a particular outcome, then it's easy to become frustrated, because you cannot control the thoughts, speech, or behavior of another person.

## 3. How do I give honest criticism to or about someone without violating Compassionate Communication?

First, check in with your own heart to find your motivation for speaking: Am I motivated by kindness and care for this person, or am I invested in getting her to change? Am I trying to make her conform to my idea of how she should be? Am I trying to change another person to avoid seeing or feeling something within myself? Can I acknowledge this is *my* perception and not some object or absolute truth? The key factor lies not in the technique but in awareness of your internal experience and your intention for speaking at all.

It may be well to ask the other person if she is interested in being critiqued. If she is not open to hearing this, true communication may never occur, no matter how skillful or compassionate your speech or writing may be.

Listen to or download the audio meditation for this practice at *unitybooks.org/living*.

# INTRODUCTION TO
# THE SPECIAL PRACTICES

Practices 1 to 5 are the Core Practices. The Core Practices together form the foundation from which we can live our lives consciously and compassionately. Our intention is for these Core Practices to be integrated into all we do, and all we are. They are open-ended: There is no limit to the depth or breadth of how they may be applied; and they can be practiced for a lifetime.

Practices 6 to 10 are called Special Practices. Refinements and special applications of the Core Practices, they are specialized practices that have a specific focus. Each practice is to be engaged for a limited period of time. Initially, do each practice in the order presented; after completing all five, you may then choose to repeat a certain practice, if you wish.

The Special Practices consist of temporarily viewing every life experience through a particular lens. Each lens provides a way through which you interpret your experiences. Each practice takes a particular perspective. These perspectives are not necessarily true in an absolute or universal sense; each one is simply a working hypothesis, which is assumed to be true for the time period designated for your practice.

The Core Practices may become permanently incorporated into your life. This is *not* the intention for the Special Practices. Ideally, each of these would be practiced for 30 days, and then you would move on to the next. Three weeks would constitute the minimum length of time necessary; anything less than that may not give you a sufficient length of time to be significantly impacted by the practice.

Each practice may be seen as a slogan that can be repeated periodically. These are not affirmations. I repeat the slogan not as an attempt to convince myself it's true, but simply to remind myself this is the lens through which I am now viewing my world. I simply assume each is true, without question, during the period designated for practice.

# 8. PRACTICE 6:
# EVERYTHING IS MY TEACHER

### What Is This Practice?

Let's look at what it means to practice Everything Is My Teacher. It means every person, place, object, event, and experience in my life is a potential teacher. My work is to learn from it. But what does it mean "to learn"?

To learn is to gain the ability to express myself in ways not possible before the learning occurred. If I learn a new language, I am able to relate to other people and other cultures in ways not previously possible. I can read more books, find more friends, and travel more freely than I could before. Learning provides the opportunity for greater freedom of expression.

Right now I am not free to play music on a piano. This is not because anyone is prohibiting me from doing this. It is because I have limited knowledge of music and have not learned to play the piano. If I were to learn more about music and learn to play the piano, then I could express myself in ways not presently possible. I would have more freedom.

To learn music and to play the piano requires discipline and practice. Practice requires effort over a sustained period of time. To do this, I need a strong intention: A deep desire and a commitment to engage the practice. At times, I might not want to do my piano practice. My intention will hopefully prevail, so I will do it in spite of my resistance. I will temporarily override my short-term desires for greater freedom of self-expression in the long run. This is called *discipline*.

We will return to the topic of discipline; but first, let's distinguish between two types of learning: conventional learning and deep learning. Conventional learning is learning something I know I don't know. I know I don't know how to play the piano. I know I don't know how to speak Russian. To learn to play the piano or to speak Russian would be a form of conventional learning. Conventional learning extends my knowledge and skills horizontally. This type of learning may broaden me considerably, but it does not necessarily *deepen* me.

Deep learning is when I learn something I didn't even know I didn't know. Deep learning takes me into a new dimension of being. It's not only going to a place I've not been to before, but it's going to a place I could not even have conceived of before. This is the nature of deep learning. It can be recognized only *after* the learning takes place; it cannot be fully understood within my existing framework of understanding. To live originally is to be fully open to deep learning every moment of my life. It means to use everything as my teacher.

Christopher Columbus sailed eastward expecting to find India. He wanted to find India to expand commercial possibilities for Europeans. There was no way for him to fully understand the implications of his discovery. He thought he found India and thus he named the natives "Indians." But, he landed in a New World, a world which was far beyond his comprehension. The consequences of his adventure were beyond the possible understanding of anyone alive at that time. As they say, the rest is history; but a history no one on earth could have predicted!

Such is the nature of deep learning, and transformation is its deepest form. It takes us places we never knew existed and opens worlds presently inconceivable. The outcome cannot be predicted; it is open-ended and without limits.

Let's return to the role of discipline in deep learning. Every spiritual practice is a form of discipline. The words "discipline" and "disciple" have the same origin. We become disciples of our own essential nature. Spiritual practice is a discipline we engage for the purpose of deep learning and transformation. It's very important to continue the practice even if it is sometimes difficult to see how discipline relates to our intentions.

In the 1984 hit movie *The Karate Kid*, "the new kid in school," Daniel (Ralph Macchio), frequently gets pummeled by a gang of boy thugs. Then one night during a routine beating, a seemingly old, frail Japanese man, "Mr. Miyagi" (Pat Morita), comes out of nowhere, quickly subdues the thugs, and saves Daniel. Daniel is astonished at Mr. Miyagi's ability to beat up a bunch of well-trained karate buffs without breaking a sweat, so he begs Mr. Miyagi to train him. Mr. Miyagi agrees. To begin, he asks Daniel to start waxing his collection of antique automobiles, using a strict, circular motion. "Wax on … wax off … wax on … wax off …" After many hours of waxing, Mr. Miyagi asks Daniel to sand the floor, and then paint a large fence … all while using strict and specific motions … "Side to side … up and down …"

Daniel protests loudly, "I came here to learn karate … not to wax cars and paint fences …" Miyagi ignores his protests and reminds him, "Wax on … wax off …" But Daniel's continued practice eventually pays off. Under Miyagi's tutelage, Daniel becomes very adept at karate and goes on to defeat the toughest, most skilled karate student in the "All-Valley Karate Tournament" championship.

This story is illustrative of spiritual practice; we may see no relationship between our daily practice and our mind's version of what we desire. We may protest and grumble, but the work is simply to "wax on, wax off …" We do the practice without looking for specific outcomes, yet we know it is leading somewhere far beyond where we are right now.

Patience and persistence are crucial; trying to "push the river" is counterproductive. Our conditioned tendency is to think if we work harder or longer, we will attain our goal more quickly. This is not so with deep learning. Effort and discipline are important, but so is patience and trust. A gentle, yet persistent practice works best.

A young man went to a Zen master and said earnestly, "I am devoted to studying Zen; how long will it take me to become enlightened?" The teacher quickly replied, "Ten years." Impatiently, the student answered, "But I want to attain it faster than that. I will work very hard. I will meditate 12 hours a day, every day. How long will it take then?" The teacher paused for a moment and then replied, "Twenty years."

Be curious, be persistent, and stay open; this is the best way to learn from everything.

## Why This Practice Is Transformative

Who you really are is infinitely more than the ego. Yet the ego, as well as the physical body, is a necessary vehicle to function as a human being on this planet. Developing a healthy ego, and a healthy body, is an essential part of spiritual development, but this is not enough because this is not all of who we are.

The ego (as well as the body) may be likened to an automobile, which is a necessity for most of us. My automobile is important to me because I need it to function in the modern world. I want it to function well, so I will give it whatever attention it needs. But I am not my automobile; I don't want to live my entire life inside it. There is much more to my life than my Honda Accord; and there is much more to me than my ego and my body.

Transformative spiritual practice does not attempt to destroy the ego, but to transcend, and include, the ego. The ego, like my automobile, is necessary and important, but it is not the entirety of who I am. As I expand self-awareness beyond the ego, it becomes more transparent, more fluid, and more functional. The ego then serves as a vehicle for essential nature rather than an obstacle to its expression.

———

To transcend ego, I need to dissolve my exclusive identification with it. Transformative spiritual practice dissolves the roots of ego-identification.

These roots are attachment, resistance, and identification with the mind. When identified with ego, I want to feel safe, I want to always be right, I want to be in control, and I want to be recognized as special and important. I resist uncertainty. I resist my authority being challenged. I resist not being recognized. My attention is on me, me, and me. Even when my attention is focused on another person, if I take an honest look at myself, I will see how I want this other person to make *me* feel safe, loved, special, and so on.

The ego is much like an adolescent who is self-absorbed with his new identity. This is a necessary part of his development, but he must grow beyond that to become a healthy adult. Our practice is not to condemn the ego but to help it grow up and discover its true purpose. It can be a wonderful servant, but it's a terrible master!

Life is our greatest teacher. Perhaps this is the reason we exist in physical form: to learn by experiencing life as it is. But when identified with ego, we are not open to learning—we are more invested in promoting and protecting our personal beliefs and opinions. The ego is not open to truth; it wants to see and hear only that which protects and supports itself.

One powerful anecdote for ego-identification is humility, but not the false humility of self-criticism or self-debasement. True humility simply sees things as they are: I am not the center of the universe; I am not the most important person in the world; I do not have all the answers. I am not bad; I simply have much to learn.

Transformative spiritual practice is a form of learning, but it's very different from conventional learning. It is not gaining more knowledge, but gaining more wisdom. To grow in wisdom requires deep emptiness, which is the best attitude for this practice. Emptiness is a deep willingness to learn.

A Japanese Zen master received a learned university professor who came to inquire about Zen. The professor introduced himself and commenced telling the Zen master how much he knew about Asian religion, Asian history, and Asian culture, but he knew relatively little about Zen, so he wanted to add this to his vast repertoire of knowledge.

The Zen master served the professor some tea. He filled the visitor's cup to overflowing and then kept pouring. The professor shouted, "Stop man; the cup is already too full!" The Zen master responded, "Like this cup, you, too, are full of your presumed knowledge. I cannot show you Zen unless you first empty your cup."

So we begin the practice by emptying our cup. We can empty our cup only when we see how full it already is! Much of this practice is seeing how full our cup is and then being willing to empty it. By seeing everything as our teacher, we begin to empty our cup. The ego will protest: "How can this person possibly teach me anything! What could I possibly learn from this situation?" See where your cup is too full. Notice these self-righteous protests, and then respond just as Mr. Miyagi would: "Wax on … Wax off."

True emptiness requires true humility, which is a deep willingness to learn. This opens us to life instead of struggling to control it. Jesus tells us the meek shall inherit the earth (Mt. 5:5). One meaning of the term *meek* is "to be teachable." Everything Is My Teacher is the practice of true humility and genuine meekness.

Wisdom teachings from many traditions throughout history tell us that openness, humility, and teachability are key factors in transformation. In ancient Greece, Socrates said, "As for me, all I know is that I know nothing."[18] And from ancient China, the Tao Te Ching tells us to "Yield and overcome; Bend and be straight; Empty and be full."[19] And in the Gospels, Jesus teaches, "Whoever becomes humble like this child is the greatest in the kingdom of heaven" (Mt. 18:4 NRSV).

## Forms of the Practice

The general practice consists of meeting each life experience with an underlying attitude of "this experience is my teacher." The essential factor is meeting each life experience with an open mind and an open heart, and with the intention of learning something about yourself. You may find it helpful to occasionally repeat the phrase, "Everything is my teacher," and you may occasionally sit for a few moments and meditate on this phrase.

It's particularly important to engage this practice when you encounter a circumstance or a person who triggers fear, judgment, or some form of resistance, or when you feel a strong attachment to a particular outcome. When it feels like "Something has gone wrong!" it may be a difficult to do the practice, but it's the *best* time to do it. Big attachment? Big resistance? Big learning opportunity!

Yet it's important to be gentle with yourself and to not try to force anything to happen. Let yourself feel what you feel; stay aware and open to what is here now, and be open to what is possible to learn. Remember, we are not performing a task or trying to accomplish something. We are just being open to learn from everything and everyone.

Formal practice consists of dedicating a period of time to do nothing but the practice itself. We may do this if we notice a particular experience triggers some strong emotions, or if an event generates strong or lingering feelings. We may also do formal practice if we feel strong resistance or attachment to a particular person.

The formal practice is that of journaling. One way to do this is to write a description of an event and your feelings about it. Read what you've written and then notice your feelings. Then take a few moments and feel the event* as if it were part of yourself; feel it physically and emotionally. Bring awareness to the experience within yourself. Do not edit, analyze, or interpret anything—just feel it. Then record your feelings.

Then begin a written dialogue with this feeling, as if you were speaking to another person. Write what you say as your "normal" self; write it as a statement or a question, and then "become the event within yourself," and respond in writing to your initial statement or question. Continue the written dialogue back and forth until it seems to complete itself. Write whatever you would like to say to this experience. Some helpful questions might be: "What do you have to say to me?" "What do you want from me?" "What gift do you have for me?" Do not edit or analyze the responses; just record them in your journal.

For example, let's say you have had an argument with a close friend and you feel upset about it. Take time to write down your description of the event and then notice your feelings about it; record these as well. Read what you've written and notice what you feel. Then take a few moments to go within and sense that person within yourself; notice how it feels.

As yourself, record a statement or question to your friend. Now, return to your "friend" as you experience him or her within yourself; feel this presence. Now respond as this presence. Do not respond as you think your friend would respond, but respond *as the presence itself*. Do not edit, analyze, or interpret; just write it down. Continue the process back and forth for as long as necessary. Take your time, be patient—and trust the process. You may need to do it a few times before it feels natural,

---

*I use the word *event* but this can also be a person, an organization, or a circumstance.

but once you do, you can find it a very effective instrument for self-awareness and healing.

An alternative form of this practice is to feel the event or person within yourself, then let yourself become that feeling, and then give it some expression. Identify with it as much as possible; then speak, sing, or scream; move your body or dance; draw, paint, or sculpt; write poetry or music; do whatever feels natural to you. Let yourself do whatever you feel like doing as long as it is not harmful to anyone. First, feel it deeply and then give it complete expression.

A variation of this practice is to sit facing an empty chair. Imagine your dialogue partner (an event or another person) is sitting in the other chair. Speak (as yourself) to the "presence" in the other chair; speak from your heart. Pause a moment and then go sit in the other chair; take a moment to "become" the presence in that chair. Then respond verbally, as that presence, to what you said. You are not talking about the event; you are speaking as if you *were* the event itself. Wait a moment and then return to the original chair and then respond as yourself. Continue this process for as long as you feel there is some energy remaining in the dialogue. When you feel complete, just sit quietly for a few moments.

We can do this for any experience, including a dream. The key is to avoid mental interpretation or control and to then feel deeply and trust the process. The teaching lies within the event itself, as we experience it internally. Both the event and the teaching lie within us; each is a vehicle for transformation if we use them wisely.

### Perils on the Path

The far enemy of this practice is to go unconscious and live in the arrogance of believing, "I already know the truth." Rarely are we that explicit, but that is the general attitude of the ego.

This occurs most commonly in the form of a fixed attitude or preoccupied mindset wherein there is no opening for new learning.

The near enemy of spiritual practice is to believe we are doing transformative work but are unwittingly feeding ego-identification.

The near enemy of this practice is to engage the practice with an intention of self-improvement or of becoming a "better person." From the perspective of transformational spirituality, we do not need to become a "better person" because our true nature is infinitely more than any self-image the mind can conjure. This work is not self-improvement, but waking up to our true nature.

I can engage this practice with the intention of accumulating knowledge I will find "useful" in my work or everyday life. One of the subtle temptations for ministers, writers, and spiritual teachers is to see every learning experience through the lens of "the next sermon" or "the next book." The motivation for doing the practice then slides into a utilitarian professional endeavor, rather than waking up spiritually. Certainly, others may benefit from my new learning, but they will benefit much more from my own spiritual awakening.

The great paradox is that when we do the practice in a transformational context, then the utilitarian payoff is still present, but as a by-product rather than the primary goal. Whatever I do, I will do it much better from an awakened state than from an unawakened one. I can accumulate knowledge from conventional learning; I can gain wisdom only by waking up to my true nature. Jesus tells us to "Strive first for the kingdom of God … and all these things will be given to you as well" (Mt. 6:33 NRSV).

## FAQ

**1. I have an issue that has been plaguing me most of my life. I have tried many times to understand what I am to learn from this—and I never get an answer!**

Two important points are to be made here. One is to remember the object of this practice is not to get an answer to a specific question or the resolution of a particular issue. We do the practice to awaken spiritually, but beyond that intention, there is no specific goal or intended outcome. We are not trying to solve a problem. Answers often will come to us, but this is always a byproduct of the practice, not our primary intention.

Second, this practice is built upon the foundational practices. Continue to practice awareness, acceptance, forgiveness, and so on, as you engage the current practice. Look to see if you are trying to get an answer because you are now experiencing something deemed "unacceptable." If so, engage the practice of deep acceptance. Also, practice Radical Self-Awareness; perhaps there is something you are not aware of that is driving your search for an answer.

**2. How can I do this practice without intellectualizing? Don't I have to identify what it is I am learning?**

Not necessarily. The practice is to cultivate an attitude of learning from every experience, person, event, and circumstance in your life. If you recognize a specific learning, great; but if not, it doesn't matter. When you do identify something you have learned, it's important not to spend a lot of time mentally "chewing" on it; just notice it and then return to the present.

The formal aspects of this practice, such as the journaling, dialogue, and so forth, are not ruminating upon what you've learned, but are practiced in order to go deeper into an experience and uncover what you may not have seen in your awareness of the original experience. Some events may be quite sudden or complex, so we may not be fully aware of all facets of the experience at the time it occurred. We "return" to the experience to engage it more deeply with awareness—not to ponder what has been learned.

**3. Is every life experience there to teach us something? Maybe things just happen! And, can't we be there to teach someone else rather than always for our own learning?**

I have no idea why things happen as they do, and asking that question is not part of this practice. The practice is to open up to every life experience with the premise it has something to teach us. Each life experience can then become a catalyst for awakening, regardless of any "objective" reason for its occurrence.

Perhaps there is no absolute answer to the question of "Why has this happened?" Any answer I have to this question depends more on my own perspective and level of understanding than anything else. In this practice, I am less interested in finding "answers" than I am in discovering my own true nature.

Yes, it is possible we may have an experience for the purpose of teaching others, but we always return to our premise that there is also something for *me* to learn; with every experience, we say, "This, too, is my teacher."

Listen to or download the audio meditation for this
practice at *unitybooks.org/living*.

# 9. PRACTICE 7:
# DANCING WITH CHAOS

## What Is This Practice?

What do you think of when you hear the word *chaos*? To most people, it means turmoil and confusion—something to be avoided or overcome as quickly as possible. Chaos in the economy, in the weather, or in world affairs may trigger fear and a sense of insecurity in some of us. We fear chaos because outcomes are unpredictable and there may be the potential great loss or harm to someone.

We typically have an aversion to mental or emotional chaos as well. This can occur when our life seems to be turned upside down by an unpredictable event, by uncertain conditions, or by the loss of something familiar. A sudden death, the ending of a relationship, or a sudden financial crisis can catapult us into a chaotic emotional state.

This response to chaos arises from our intention to maintain the status quo, to retain that which is familiar and apparently safe. This is normal for most of us. But safety and stability is not always possible—and it may not even be desirable. There are many potentialities inherent within chaos; if we are unwilling to experience chaos, we may be avoiding the opportunity for transformation. If we are seeking transformation, then we must find a new and more creative way of relating to chaos: We must learn how to dance with it!

Let's begin by examining the etymology of the word. The English *chaos* is derived from the Greek *khaos*. One definition of *khaos* is "formless primordial space," which refers to the great void that preceded the creation of the universe in the Greek creation myths. Khaos was a great, yawning nothingness; an abyss of infinite size. Out of this void emerged Gaia, the Earth goddess. Gaia symbolizes the world of form and structure, in contrast to the unformed chaos. This world of form is the one with which we usually identify and cling to.

Considering chaos as formless primordial space, we look at the word "primordial." In the science of biology, *primordial* means "relating to the earliest stage of development of an organism." Chaos may be seen as the earliest stage of the formation of a new life. The word *primordial* is derived from the Latin *primordium*, which means "original." To live originally is to live from this primordial ground of infinite possibility, which is the very source of life itself.

Gaia, the world of form, arose out of chaos. The form arises (without explanation) from the formless primordium. To this day, science has no explanation whatever as to how or why everything in the universe was created out of nothing at all—in one Big Bang. Perhaps, it is the nature of this universe to create the formed from the unformed, in every dimension of existence.

Chaos is not just turmoil or confusion; it is also the unformed and unborn potential for new life. Chaos is the precursor of creation; all worlds are born from chaos. When form is destroyed, chaos ensues, and eventually from chaos new forms will emerge; this is the ongoing process of evolution. All creation is born from chaos. When you allow yourself to consciously enter this primordial state, you come to the place where all worlds are born; and you become a cocreator.

Creativity is itself a chaotic process. All transformative spiritual practice is a form of creativity; it is dancing with chaos. The German philosopher Friedrich Nietzsche said, "One must have a chaos inside oneself to give birth to a dancing star."[20] By consciously entering the realm of chaos, you enter into the dance of creation; and a star is born!

In the wonderful story *Zorba the Greek,* a reserved English businessman named Basil sails to Crete on a business venture, and on the voyage he encounters the embodiment of his un-lived life in the form of an old Greek named Zorba. Whereas the Englishman lived a controlled, well-planned, and respectable life, Zorba is a wanderer, a drinker, a womanizer, a poet, and a dancer. Zorba revels in life; he loves what he terms "the full catastrophe of life."

Zorba goes to work for Basil and quickly brings chaos into his life. Yet he gradually teaches the nervous Englishman to em-brace all of it. The business venture collapses (in no small mea-sure due to Zorba's antics) and the story ends with an iconic scene that takes place on a secluded beach. There, Zorba teaches the Englishman how to dance; and they dance together with abandon amidst the ruins of their disastrous business venture.

We don't necessarily have to emulate Zorba's lifestyle, but we can learn from his indomitable spirit of openness, resilience, nonattachment, and love for "the full catastrophe" of life!

To dance, we must flow with the rhythm of the music. To dance with chaos, we must meet it with nonresistance and flow with its rhythm. We learn to recognize the rhythm underlying the chaos and then flow with it. Morihei Ueshiba, originator of the Japanese martial art of Aikido, says, "Every moment is etched with nature's grand design—do not try to deny or op-pose the cosmic order of things."[21] Beneath all chaos is an un-derlying pattern of emergence. This pattern is the genome for the new life seeking to be born. Dancing With Chaos—which is somewhat like practicing Aikido—is learning to recognize and resonate with that emergent pattern.

Within the past 50 years, a new form of mathematics known as Chaos Theory has emerged into prominence. This theory shows some deterministic systems are still inherently unpre-dictable due to minute variations in the initial conditions. Even the tiniest error in estimating an initial condition can render a theoretically predictable outcome to become highly unpredictable.* But "unpredictable" does not mean without order. Chaotic systems are unpredictable, but not without order—they are not random. Chaotic systems contain hidden patterns. The force that gives shape to these patterns is known as an *attractor*.

Our life experiences may be likened to a chaotic system: They are unpredictable, but are they patterned. This pattern is shaped by an attractor, and that attractor is *intention*. Our intentions pattern our lives, but they do not do it deterministically. We cannot predict exactly what will arise in our life experience, but we can know it is patterned by the underlying power of intention.

The practice of Dancing With Chaos begins with the intention to dance with chaos for the purpose of creating a new life. Hold this intention during the course of your everyday life and look for opportunities to dance with chaos when it emerges. Begin to recognize chaos as it arises. Look at those experiences of disappointment, disruption, or uncertainty. Chaos occurs when mental forms such as beliefs, assumptions, and expectations are challenged and disrupted. The deeper the disruption, the deeper the chaos we experience.

Recognize your response to these experiences. Feel your emotions, look at your thoughts, feel the sensations in your body. Begin with awareness, and then acceptance. Ask yourself, *Can I welcome this experience as a symptom of a deeper reality seeking birth? Am I open to a greater reality emerging through this experience?*

A key factor is to consciously surrender to the process. This does not mean resignation; and it does not mean living aimlessly. Conscious surrender means entering into the process of

---

*In theory, even an undetected butterfly flapping its wings can disturb conditions in a global weather system such that accurate long-range prediction is rendered impossible. This is the origin of the oft-quoted term, "The Butterfly Effect."

creative chaos with a clear intention for transformation. As you do this, you will see the universe itself is attempting to evolve through you!

Harmonize yourself with this emerging flow of universal creativity; become a conscious cocreator, and you will forever be creating new worlds without any effort. In the Tao Te Ching, it is written:

> The Tao of heaven does not strive,
> and yet it overcomes.
> It does not speak, and yet it is answered.
> It does not ask, yet it is supplied with all its needs.
> It seems at ease, and yet it follows a plan.[22]

Watch for chaos as it arises, bow to it, greet it as a new dance partner, listen to its silent music, and feel its rhythm in your body. Let the intention for transformation be the attractor that shapes your life experiences, and then step onto the dance floor!

In the summer of 1986, I was married and serving as the senior minster in a medium-sized suburban church in an affluent Midwestern community. From the outside, everything appeared to be going great. By the spring of 1988, all of this had come to an end. Divorced, broke, and without a job or a career, I entered into a period of chaos that reflected itself in every arena of my life. I was in a free-fall. Eventually, I learned to make friends with the chaos. Psychotherapy, Native American spiritual practices, a Buddhist meditation practice, and my involvement in a men's spiritual movement all taught me how to dance with the chaos; each contributed a unique perspective, and each had its own movement in the dance.

I created a new intention for my life and began to live from that intention. A new life gradually emerged; certainly not one I consciously orchestrated, but clearly one that reflected my deepest desires. The new life was not only in regard to external conditions, but more important, a new internal life emerged that was not even fathomable in my prior circumstances. This new life includes a continuous process of evolution and self-renewal; the transformation continues—it is far from complete!

## Why This Practice Is Transformative

To the infant, life is pure chaos: It is but a collage of sensations, sounds, and images. Gradually a self, an ego, forms that gives some order and meaning to this jumbled array of experiences. This ego formation is necessary for the child to function in the world of time, space, and form, and it is a necessary part of our spiritual development.

Sometimes the chaos is too frightening or too painful, so the child will develop a strong resistance to the chaos. Chaos becomes associated with fear and pain rather than adventure and aliveness. The ego structure will then become rigid, inflexible, and brittle rather than organic and protean. This rigidity can seem necessary for survival and may serve us well in our family origin. However, this rigidity is not necessary to functioning as an adult, and it may even become quite problematic for ourselves or for others.

Based upon our personal history, each ego develops, at its core, a fixated belief about itself and the world, as well as a strategy for getting its needs met. For example, one ego may be fixated on the belief that the world is a harsh and dangerous place. He decides, "I must be strong and aggressive to survive." Another ego may be fixated on the same belief, but may develop a different strategy, such as, "I must hide and be invisible to survive." Yet another ego may fixate on a different core belief, such as, "Love is scarce, conditional, and must be earned." One strategy for coping with this is, "I must be 'good' and please others to get the love I need." Other fixations and other strategies abound; they define the roles and the scripts we unconsciously play out in our everyday lives.

---

Referring to chaos theory and to the attractor that shapes the pattern of events, we can see the fixation as the attractor that shapes the pattern of our thoughts, emotions, behaviors, and relationships throughout our lives. Our life circumstances will inevitably reflect this attractor pattern. Intellectual understanding and willpower does not automatically change this, because the fixation is not just another thought we choose to entertain; it is the core of our identity. To surrender this feels like annihilation. The philosopher Karlfried Graf Durckheim writes, "Only to the extent that we expose ourselves over and over again to annihilation can that which is indestructible arise within us."[23] Only when we are willing to allow the ego to be annihilated will we see we are so much more than just the ego.

Chaos carries the potential for transformation because it challenges our identification with ego; it challenges the ego's very existence. However, that which is real cannot be annihilated. Your true nature is indestructible. And, you don't really lose the ego; you simply lose your identification with it. The ego then becomes more fluid and transparent; it now serves as a vehicle for your true nature to express rather than an obstacle to its expression.

What does get lost is your exclusive identification with the ego. This may feel like annihilation, even though it is quite the opposite. It is not death, but the awakening to your true life. When we are identified with the ego, it is much like a caterpillar; it must experience dissolution so its true nature as the butterfly can emerge. To the extent we try to keep the caterpillar in its present form, we are delaying the emergence of the butterfly. We can never force disidentification with ego because the very attempt to do so reinforces ego-identification, and delays transformation. This process of transformation is one of nonstop surrender—which includes letting go of all attempts to orchestrate the process of surrender itself.

———

## Forms of the Practice

To dance with chaos, we must recognize it and notice any resistance we have to it. Chaos arises more often than we might realize. It arises whenever we enter into the unknown, the uncertain, or the unstructured. When we fall asleep at night, we enter the world of chaos. Rather than seeing sleep as just recharging our battery so we can prepare for another day of busyness, we can choose to enter into and return from the sleep state with an attitude of openness and curiosity. Notice how you feel as you fall asleep, and then again as you awaken. Notice what has changed.

Chaos can be very creative. Dreams arise from the formless primordial (and potentially creative) space we call sleep. If you have questions or issues you take into sleep, notice your awareness of these as you awaken in the morning. Recall the dreams you can remember; how do you feel about these dream memories? See them as teachers, even if you do not have a clue what they mean!

It's quite interesting to see the relationship between chaos and creativity. Creativity requires a period of chaos, which forms the fertile void from which new life expressions arise. Every teaching on creativity I have encountered encourages us to begin by letting go of all assumptions and expectations before engaging the process. Being willing to enter the "don't know" space opens us to chaos, which is the potential for new life. This introduces us to living originally.

Periods of chaos in our life can be opportunities to see life in a whole new context. Filmmaker Greg Colbert writes, "Ever since my house burned down, I see the moon more clearly."[24] Periods of chaos can be ways of "burning down" those parts of the psyche that may be familiar and comforting, but also limit our full experience of life. We can choose to see chaos as the potential for freedom rather than as an unfortunate disaster.

---

You need not wait for a major disaster to clear your mind and heart; you can use life's "mini-disasters" for this purpose. Anytime your plans are disrupted, something is lost, or expectations thwarted, you can use these as openings to a new vista on life. How do you relate to these experiences? Do they trigger anger or fear? Do you see them as obstacles? It's okay to feel your disappointment, anger, or grief when these disruptions occur, *but don't stop there.* You can see these emotions as part of the creative process itself; be present to the experiences in your mind and body. What would it be like to open up and "dance" with these experiences?

Chaos can arise solely as an internal experience, with no apparent external trigger. The times we feel anxious, depressed, or agitated, we can simply be present without suppressing, analyzing, or medicating these feelings—and without identifying with them as well. See these experiences as you would view a stormy sky. Like a great thunderstorm, it's possible to see the power and the beauty concealed within these experiences. Remember the feeling of aliveness you've had after a big storm has just past, when even the air itself feels charged with new life?

The formal practice of Dancing With Chaos can take a number of forms. One is to journal or dialogue with an experience of chaos. You can dialogue with it, following the process described in the previous chapter. Choose something you have experienced as chaos, such as a loss, a disappointment, or a disruption of your plans.

As you recall the event or circumstances, notice your response to it. Notice your thoughts, emotions, desires, and physical sensations. Notice if there is any craving or resistance present. Dialogue with the event as you experience it right now. Refrain from analysis, interpretation, and judgment as much as possible. Converse with the event as if it were an entity, with its own life and its own intelligence. Keep records of your dialogues over a period of time—you may see a pattern emerge that is not evident in a single dialogue.

The events of our lives may have no final meaning—they are organic and open-ended. It may be helpful to revisit some of them from time to time. The meaning you discover in an event may change as *you* change over time. In a sense, the past *does* change, because each time you view it with new eyes, the meaning of it will change.

In the practice of meditation, we consciously embrace chaos. Many people think of meditation as a way of escaping chaos, but don't enter meditation with the intention of escaping anything! True meditation is about opening up to, facing, and embracing *every* experience with a clear mind and an open heart.

In meditation practice, we step out of the formed world of our thoughts and beliefs. We let go of our usual patterns of reaction and defense; we let go of the world as we know it to be, and we enter into the direct experience of life *as it is* in this very moment. This is like jumping into Alice's rabbit hole—we enter a strange new world! As we persevere in our practice, we find that in the heart of our ever-changing experience lies that which never changes: our own essential nature. As we learn to dance with our chaos, we discover the place within us that is forever undisturbed; we find the *still point*:

> At the still point of the turning world. Neither flesh nor fleshless; Neither from nor towards; at the still point, there the dance is, But neither arrest nor movement. And do not call it fixity, Where past and future are gathered. Neither movement from nor towards, Neither ascent nor decline. Except for the point, the still point, There would be no dance, and there is only the dance …[25]

The dance itself occurs in the world of time, space, and form; the still point exists only in the only eternal present, which is beyond time and space itself. Paradoxically, these exist simultaneously, and they depend upon each other. We can experience the still point in the midst of the dance. We can experience the timeless while active in the world of time and space. This is what it means to "be in the world, but not of it." This is what it means to live originally.

## Perils on the Path

The far enemy of Dancing With Chaos is attempting to deny or suppress the experience of chaos; it is refusing to allow chaos to emerge. One symptom of this is the addiction to always feeling in control. If you have this tendency, then whenever you start to feel out of control, allow yourself to experience the underlying feelings. Most often, it will be fear. Stay present to the fear and to whatever emotion follows—it may be anger, shame, loneliness, or grief. Experience these emotions in your body. You may discover a belief underlies the emergent emotions. Memories may arise. Underlying the resistance may be an unhealed wound that has been activated by a current event or circumstance. Allow all of this to emerge and stay present to the sensations in your body.

Michelle came to me for spiritual counseling. She said she was dreadfully afraid of chaos; particularly in the form of disagreements or interpersonal conflict. She would panic at the slightest indication of conflict arising. After counseling with her awhile, Michelle recalled that in her family of origin, a disagreement would usually lead to an argument, which would then lead to intense shouting, and sometimes even violence. She recalled being very young and very frightened when this occurred. As an adult, whenever she encountered any form of conflict, she would once again feel very young and very frightened. Seeing the origin of her fear of conflict allowed her to eventually move beyond it.

Violence and abusive behavior are not the same as chaos in the true sense of the word. Such behavior is more likely a *resistance* to chaos. Chaos is the unformed, the unknown. Experiencing chaos often means feeling out of control. Resistance to this experience can sometimes take the form of violence. Disagreement and interpersonal conflict can be chaotic, but disagreement and conflict are *not* inherently bad, and do *not* need to lead to violence. If handled skillfully, a disagreement can lead to a breakthrough in understanding for those on both sides of the argument.

Michelle did not actually fear chaos itself; she feared the abusive behavior in her family that arose when chaos attempted to emerge. Chaos itself was not the problem; the violent refusal to experience chaos was the real problem. She began to see this distinction and then allowed herself to feel the emotions and physical sensations underlying the fear and resistance. By seeing her fear had its roots in the past, and by staying with her present moment experience, the fear eventually disappeared. She then learned to use experiences of disagreement and confusion as opportunities to learn about herself. This greatly enriched her relationships and her experience of life. Resistance, met with awareness, is an opportunity to heal, and to live more freely and powerfully in the world.

A near enemy of Dancing With Chaos is to equate it with indecisiveness or an unwillingness to make a commitment or take a stand on anything. Some individuals seem to live in a perpetual state of uncertainty, which is based upon an unwillingness to stand for, or against, anything. They may have an "anything goes" or "whatever you want" approach to life that can masquerade as flexibility or equanimity—but it is not. Living in a muddle of indecisiveness is not the same as Dancing With Chaos!

Brandon came for counseling with the issue of what he described as "terminal wishy-washiness." He referred to himself as the "consummate chameleon." He would take the shape of whatever he felt someone else wanted. He finally realized this was creating a big problem for himself, as well as for his partner, and many of his friends.

By exploring his personal history, Brandon began to see, as a child, whenever he verbalized his own thoughts or feelings, he would be ridiculed or humiliated, if not by his parents, then by his older siblings. Being the youngest in the family, he often took the brunt of the disowned hostility that seemed to permeate the family system. His survival strategy was to "never give them a target" by never taking a firm stand on anything. By seeing this, and being willing to experience his feelings in the reality of the present, Brandon was eventually able to dissolve the fear of humiliation that arose every time he stood up for himself. He became clearer about what *he* really wanted and more confident in his own beliefs.

Dancing With Chaos means we are willing to live with uncertainty when it's inherent in our circumstances *and* we are able to make decisions and commitments as appropriate. To dance, we must be able to stand on our own two feet. To Dance With Chaos means we are not afraid of chaos, nor are we afraid of forming appropriate boundaries.

A similar near enemy is mistaking uproar and drama for Dancing With Chaos. Some individuals live in a constant sea of conflict and confusion; and if it isn't present now, then they find a way to make it happen! There may be many reasons why one might do this; it may be a comfort zone for some, and for others, it can be a way of getting attention. Whatever the reason, it is important to notice if we have any tendency to "play the drama."

If you tend to do this, then just notice what you experience in mind and body when you don't act out the drama. Perhaps a sense of loneliness or boredom will arise if there isn't a lot of drama in your life. When I was in psychotherapy years ago, I became aware in my family of origin the best way (and sometimes the only way) to get my parents' attention was to be in some type of crisis. I then began to see how often I played this pattern out in my life. To not be in a crisis felt very lonely at first, but I discovered those feelings would not last forever, and it was much more satisfying to live my life authentically than dramatically.

Anyone can get on the dance floor and jump around, but real dancing requires some skill; and that skill is born out of one's practice. To skillfully Dance With Chaos requires self-awareness, self-acceptance, and self-discipline. Every moment of our lives is an opportunity for practice!

**FAQ**

**1. Aren't science, social progress, and civilization themselves products of humanity's overcoming chaos?**

It depends upon what you mean by "overcoming chaos." Science tries to understand the natural world (which appears chaotic) and technology is a way of manipulating and (to a degree) controlling the natural world. Social order and civilization seem to work better than complete anarchy. But science, technology, and civilization do not work best by trying to overcome chaos, but rather by balancing chaos with a degree of order and form.

If we see knowledge and order as being at war with chaos, then we will see stress and conflict in our lives. But if order and understanding arise from working with chaos to bring about a state of balance, then we are Dancing With Chaos in a skillful way. Then, when form and understanding break down (which is inevitable), we won't see it as something "gone wrong," but rather as an opportunity to dance with the unknown and to develop new knowledge and create new forms.

**2. How do I know if some chaos in my life is natural or if I might be unconsciously causing it?**

There may be no "one size fits all" answer to this question, but generally speaking, just look at how your life is working— or *not* working. Are you experiencing resistance, suffering, or disharmony? These are not the same as chaos; they may be arising as resistance to chaos. Anytime you experience stress or suffering, look for resistance. If it is present, then there's probably some unrecognized, and most likely, unconscious factor at work. Resistance can appear in many guises: Fear, anger, and judgment are very common forms. When dancing isn't fun anymore, then maybe we aren't really dancing!

Chaos is the natural arising of the unknown, the unformed, the uncertain; it is the natural "falling apart" of that which has been formed. Remember, chaos is not necessarily the same as conflict, disharmony, or adversity; these experiences are typically the result of our resistance to chaos.

It is very important to include the Core Practices as you Dance With Chaos. The journaling and dialogue processes described in the previous chapter may also be helpful at times. Hold the intention for transformation, and trust your intuition; let these become your primary guides on your journey.

**3. Aren't physical and mental illnesses forms of chaos? Aren't health and sanity the result of eliminating chaos?**

Perhaps not; research suggests mental illness, which may appear chaotic, is actually the reverse. Mental illness occurs when the sense of self becomes rigid and closed, which restricts an open and creative response to the world.[26] Likewise, physical health requires a certain degree of chaos in the body. For example, the normal, healthy heartbeat appears to be slightly chaotic; physicians have determined when a heartbeat becomes rigidly fixed and regular, this is a sign of an impending problem.[27]

Without a certain degree of chaos, there is a loss of resilience and the capacity to respond to changes in one's life. Research suggests health—be it in mind, body, family, or society—depends upon the right mix of order and chaos. In other words … it's a dance!

Listen to or download the audio meditation for this practice at *unitybooks.org/living*.

# 10. PRACTICE 8:
# DEATH IS MY ADVISOR

## What Is This Practice?

I will introduce you to this practice via the following quotation:

> "Death is our eternal companion. It is always at our left, at an arm's length … It has always been watching you … It always will until the day it taps you."[28] These words penetrated deep into Carlos' body, giving him a feeling of nausea. Don Juan continued, "The thing to do when you're impatient is to turn to your left and ask advice from your death. An immense amount of pettiness is dropped … if you catch a glimpse of it, or if you just have the feeling that your companion is there watching you."[29]
>
> Carlos is plunged into a deep feeling of terror. Don Juan continues, "Death is the only wise advisor we have. Whenever you feel … that everything is going wrong and you're about to be annihilated, turn to your death and ask if that is so. Your death will tell you that you're wrong; that nothing really matters outside its touch."[30]

The above narrative was written by Carlos Castaneda, a young graduate student who journeyed to Mexico in the 1960s to do research on psychedelic plants. Along the way he discovered Don Juan Matus, a Yaqui Indian sorcerer who became his mentor and introduced Castaneda to a world far beyond his understanding.

Don Juan's words shook Castaneda to his core. This reaction is very normal for anyone who comes fully face-to-face with his own death. We are most uncomfortable looking at death in a personal sense; we find many ways to deny it, deflect it, or project it. I believe this is especially true in today's Western culture.

When we cannot completely deny death, we euphemize it; we do anything to avoid using the "D word" itself. Someone has "passed on," "made their transition," "gone to a better place," or "are with the Lord" … but they seldom *die*. As soon as someone "passes on," we ship the body off to some people who never knew him, and they attempt to make him look alive and ready for a night on the town.

In our denial of death, we have depersonalized it. Death has become trivialized and inconsequential; it is a common part of our entertainment fare. By the time the average American child finishes elementary school, he will have witnessed 8,000 murders on TV, and many more in the movies and in video games.[31] But none of this happens to anyone he knows; he is entirely unaffected by death—it happens only to others. If death does become quite personal and undeniable, then we view it as something "gone terribly wrong," as something that "should not be happening."

Death is the ultimate form of chaos; it is the greatest of the unknowns, it is the ultimate experience beyond our control. As such, it is our deepest avoidance. We may attempt to mitigate our fear of death with a belief about where we "go" when we die. "Yes, my body may die, but 'I' will survive intact and unscathed; 'I' will go to heaven, or reincarnate into another body, or migrate to a distant galaxy."

The great paradox in this is any of these statements may very well be true! It may be true "I" as a soul or spiritual essence survive what appears to be a death. However, if I use this belief to avoid coming fully to grips with any physical reality in my life—including death—then I am engaging what author Robert A. Masters calls a "spiritual bypass." Among many other things, this means I am using a belief *about* something to avoid having the actual experience of its truth.* Whether our belief is "true" or not is irrelevant; the problem is we are using a belief to avoid an experience. We are mistaking the menu for the meal!

When I was a youngster taking swimming lessons at the local YMCA, the instructor kept encouraging me to jump into the deep end of the pool. He would constantly assure me the water would keep me afloat. I would coyly smile and say, "Yes, I believe you totally … I have no need to jump in to prove it … I really believe you."

Of course, he saw right through my ploy, and he called my bluff! He challenged me to come out onto the end of a diving board and jump into the deep part of the pool. As I arrived at the end of the board, I felt my stomach tie into a knot and my knees lock up. He said, "You said you know you will float … so go ahead … jump in!" Frozen like a deer in headlights, I responded, "Yes, I know … but my belly doesn't!" (His further reassurance seemed to relax me enough that I eventually jumped in.)

Yes, we know we will die, but perhaps our belly doesn't quite want to go along with "knowing." We have an instinctual fear of death that lies beneath our deepest beliefs, and it can trump these beliefs in a heartbeat!

All animals fear death when they are threatened—this is part of their survival instinct. This fear is functional: Some instinctive action is taken in an attempt to survive. When the threat is removed, the fear is gone; their response to the threat ceases and they return to the business of living.

---

*For a full exploration of this topic, see Robert A. Masters, *Spiritual Bypassing: When Spirituality Disconnects Us From What Really Matters* (Berkeley, CA: North Atlantic, 2010).

Humans generally fear death differently than other animals. Humans may fear death even when there is no imminent danger or threat. Few people can reflect upon their own death—or perhaps even talk about it—without feeling a certain anxiety. Our hidden fear of death can haunt us in many ways. Underpinning every fear of loss is the fear of the greatest of all losses: the loss of our own body.

To the ego, death is the ultimate enemy. To the soul seeking freedom, death is the ultimate advisor. Repeating the words of Don Juan: "Whenever you feel that everything is going wrong and you're about to be annihilated, turn to your death and ask if that is so; your death will tell you that nothing really matters outside its touch."

I invite you to make a list of all your cares and concerns, issues and problems; all the things that are in the way of your life as you believe it "should be." Then ask, "How many of these would be problems if I had but three days to live?" And then ask, "What *would be* important to me if I had but a few days to live?" With this simple exercise you may catch a glimpse of the wisdom of using death as your advisor and the powerful impact it can have on your life!

In 1998 I joined about 30 friends in an experimental project wherein we each imagined we had only one year to live.* At our first meeting we declared our hypothetical "deathday" to be exactly one year from the present date, and we planned for each of us to develop a mock memorial service and present it to the group on that date. We then met monthly, and at the end of each meeting, we would determine what our focus would be for the next meeting. Some of the topics discussed at these meetings were:

- What do I fear most about dying?

---

*This project was based upon Stephen Levine's excellent book, *A Year to Live* (New York: Random House, 1997).

- Who and what will I miss the most when I die?
- What is important for me to finish before I die?
- What legacy do I want to leave to humanity when I die?
- What do I want shared in my obituary … in my eulogy … in my epitaph?

Far from being an exercise in morbidity, it was one of the most transforming experiences of my life. I found myself living each day at a profound depth and with a new sense of gratitude. I became crystal clear on my priorities and my values. I took nothing for granted; I left nothing unfinished. I sifted through every facet of my life, embracing it and releasing it all. Death was my advisor, and my constant companion. It has been a wise and powerful teacher for me!

I was not unique in this regard; most of my practice partners shared similar experiences. We certainly would agree with these words of Raphael Cushnir, author of *Setting Your Heart on Fire*, "Embracing your mortality makes every moment extraordinary. It quickens your entire being. It opens you more than almost anything else can … The more you bow to death, it turns out, the more you come to life."[32]

### Why This Practice Is Transformative

Transformative spiritual practice gradually eliminates identification with the ego. When we are identified with the ego, the process of disidentification feels like we're dying. In one sense, all transformative practice is about facing death; although the death referred to is generally not physical death, but rather a psychological death. And yet, to anyone identified with the ego, it feels as if there is very little difference. Whether it is death of the ego or death of the body, it feels like "*I* am dying."

In the Gospel stories, time and again Jesus admonishes his disciples to "leave everything" and to follow the Way. And "everything" does not mean just material possessions, but *every-*

*thing:* Everything you have, everything you know, and everything you believe yourself to be. This is a pretty good description of what death is.

Physical death is the most powerful symbol for "leaving everything." When we physically die, we leave everything we take to be "me and mine." We leave all our possessions, all our relationships, all our knowledge, and all our self-identifications. Although this practice ostensibly addresses physical death, in reality it goes far beyond. To face physical death fully, without denial, is to face the end of ego-identification.

The ego exists only in relation to time, space, and form. To the ego, who "I am" is always in relationship to (and in comparison with) someone or something else. The ego is my identity in the world. Without this identity in the world, the ego cannot exist. For most of us, the ego is our *exclusive* identification; if it is gone, it feels as if "I" don't exist.

How can I prove this is not true? Only by calling its bluff! "Let's see if it is true that I don't exist when the ego disappears." How can I make the ego (seem to) disappear? One way is to face and accept my own death.

Don Juan says, "Whenever you feel that you're about to be annihilated, turn to your death and ask if that is so. Your death will tell you that you're wrong." To reiterate Durckheim, "Only to the extent that we expose ourselves over and over again to annihilation can that which is indestructible arise within us." This same theme is echoed by the character of Jesus in the rock opera, *Jesus Christ Superstar,* when he sees, "To conquer death, you only have to die."[33]

Only when we are willing to allow the ego to be annihilated do we begin to see we are *much* more than the ego. What we really are is beyond any description because our true nature is boundless and indefinable. As long as we are physically alive and conscious, the ego is not permanently lost. What *does* get lost is our exclusive identification with the ego. The ego itself then ceases to be an obstruction and becomes a vehicle for our essential nature to express itself more fully in the world.

Facing your death may feel like annihilation, but in reality it is quite the opposite. It is not death, but the awakening to your true life. When identified with the ego, we are very much like the caterpillar gorging itself on its environment. And, like the caterpillar, we must experience the appearance of death so our true nature can have its wings.

Like death, ego-disidentification is a process. We may proceed through denial and anger and bargaining before we come to acceptance. In her book *The Grace in Dying*, author Kathleen Dowling Singh beautifully describes a profound similarity between the process of dying and the process of spiritual transformation.[34] In neither of these are we in charge of the process itself; but our relationship to the process is of paramount importance. The nature and quality of this relationship is entirely our choosing.

### Forms of the Practice

Begin the practice by hypothesizing a certain number of days left to live. I recommend setting your hypothetical death date as the last day of your designated practice period; but you can also set the date beyond the end of your practice period so you would finish the practice period with some days remaining. Be sure to make the death date close enough so that you will feel a certain sense of urgency as you employ the practice. If you are working with a group, it's generally best if each person in the group is working with the same date.

As you wake up each morning, become keenly aware you are one day closer to your death (which is always true). As you go about your day, hold the awareness of death as your advisor in the back of your mind. As you encounter the people in your life, experience them as if you had a limited number of days left to live. "How would I respond to this person if I had just x days left to live?" You don't necessarily have to tell them what you are doing; just notice your attitude and feelings as you relate to this person through this particular lens. This can be a very interesting experience!

As you engage in your work, play, and daily activities, relate to each activity in the very same way. Notice the attitude you have as you engage each project or task. Notice what you are aware of as you see everything from this new perspective.

When you encounter moments of stress or difficulty, stop, take a breath, "turn to your left and consult with your advisor." Perhaps you can even imagine "death" off to your left—at arm's length. Listen to what it has to say to you. Don't be concerned if you don't "hear" anything; this practice works beneath the radar of conscious awareness. Listen intuitively; listen beyond words. The very fact you have asked is a guarantee you are, in some way, being answered.

Live your external life as you normally would. Don't necessarily try to modify your behavior. Make plans and decisions as you normally do. After a while, you may find some behavior changing organically, with no conscious effort on your part. If this happens, just notice it. Don't try to control, analyze, or interpret these changes.* Just pay attention with a nonattached curiosity.

However, as you engage this practice for a while, you may feel the need to complete some personal matters. If it seems like the wise thing to do, go ahead and tend to these matters. In our practice group, a few individuals updated wills and completed some personal business matters. Some of us felt the need to share some long-held (and unspoken) thoughts and feelings

---

*Except when behavior is harmful to you or to another person; then behavior modification is essential.

with family or close friends. A few people gave away some of their prized possessions—and did so with great joy! Some folks created a "bucket list" of things they wanted to do before they (really) died. All of this is great, and none of it is required. The most important part of this practice is internal; it's about how you live your life each moment.

There are several forms of the formal practice. You may keep a journal and spend some time each day recording your experiences and insights. Record these without undue editing, analyzing, or interpreting. Pay special attention to your dreams and include them in your journal. Periodically review your journal entries and notice what you feel as you do so.

You can dialogue with death. (See Chapter 8 for a description of the dialogue process.) You can do this in the journal form, where you record each side of the dialogue in writing. Be sure to take your time and to stay connected to your feelings; do not become too analytical or editorial in this process.

You can also dialogue with death using the empty chair process. Here, you have two chairs facing each other; you sit in one and "death" sits in the other. You begin the process by speaking to the entity in the other chair, and then after a brief pause, sit in that chair, and respond *as that entity*. Once again, it is very important to stay connected to your feelings; and to stay aware of your body.

You can also "become" death and then let it speak or paint or dance. Stay present to your thoughts and feelings as you do this. Do not edit, analyze, or interpret these experiences right away. It may be helpful to do this at a later date, but for now, just let it speak for itself.

If you're working with a group, then an important part of the practice is sharing your experiences with others, as well as hearing about their experiences and insights. This can be a very rich experience, but it's important we not get too comparative or too analytical. As you listen and share with other group members, it's very important to stay aware of your own thoughts, emotions, and physical sensations. It's all about self-awareness.

## Perils on the Path

The far enemy of each practice is that which is diametrically opposed to the intention of the practice itself. The far enemy of this practice is *denial* in all its various forms. One form of denial is forgetting to do the practice, or constantly finding other things take priority over engaging the practice. Yes, there are genuine crises that can arise—but be very suspicious of any excuse to avoid or delay the practice.

A milder form of denial is engaging the practice but discounting or dismissing it in subtle ways. A common expression of this is to joke about it or to laugh it off: "Well, I don't need to pay this bill because I will be dead by the time it is due … ha, ha." This may be a subtle way of dismissing the intention of the practice through feigned humor. Certainly we don't need to be heavy-handed or glum about this; we can do this practice with a light heart and a smile, but that's very different from discounting or dismissing it. If you do find this urge to "shrug it off," then look for a hidden fear or some other form of resistance surreptitiously at work.

Also, I would encourage you to not tell unsympathetic friends or family members you are engaged in this practice. The bewildered or dismissive reactions of others will not serve to support your practice. If you wish to share with someone whom you believe will understand and be supportive, then it's certainly okay to do so; but I would advise using great discretion in your sharing with others outside your practice group.

The near enemy is that which can look like the practice, but really isn't. Some forms of the near enemy of this practice are: despair, resignation, or depression. These feelings may arise as we do this practice, but it is very important not to identify with them or to become seduced by them.

It's not unusual for this practice to uncover some unresolved grief one may have carried for a long time. Sometimes depression and despair do accompany grief—but they are definitely not the same thing. Grief is a response to some loss in our life. This may be a loss of something we had, or it may be the recognition of something we never had, but needed or deeply wanted. Grief is processed by feeling it; by feeling the emotions and the sensations in the body.

Grief is primarily an emotional process; it's an emotion that frequently changes form. Depression and despair have a quality of rigidity and flatness that does not exist in simple grief. Depression often carries the quality of hopelessness; simple grief does not. If you are aware of an enduring experience of hopelessness or despair, then it's important to explore the underlying beliefs and self-talk holding this in place. If this feeling is persistent, it may be helpful to consult with a mental health professional.

For example, a young child may experience the death of a parent. To the child this is very painful, frightening, and confusing. In an attempt to cope with these feelings, the child may conclude "anyone I love will leave me." This sets up a pattern of perpetual hopelessness and inhibits completion of the grief process. Many decades later this person may feel chronically depressed even though her external life seems to be working smoothly. The work involved for this person is to uncover the hidden belief and then complete the grieving process.

Any spiritual practice (and this one in particular) can uncover buried emotions and unresolved grief issues. If this occurs, then be sure to engage the practices of self-awareness, self-acceptance, and forgiveness. Uncovering this buried grief can lead to a very deep healing, but sometimes we can get stuck in a concealed belief that inhibits completing the grief process. As with any of these practices, if your emotions become overwhelming or debilitating, seek professional help immediately.

Having discussed the near and far enemies of spiritual practice, we might even identify a "middle enemy" of our practice as some type of resistance that lies between these two. In the current practice, it may be having the belief you are earnestly engaging the practice, but doing so only at the mental level, without experiencing the associated feelings. This can be a subtle form of denial. Some symptoms of this may be: getting lost in the "drama" of dying; talking too much about it; or feeling some sense of pride or accomplishment in doing the practice. This is where other group members or a spiritual director can give us some helpful feedback. Spiritual companionship is an important part of this journey, especially if our companions are not only supportive but also completely honest with us.

## FAQ

### 1. Thoughts are creative; might I be causing my death by dwelling on it?

Thoughts are creative if we believe they are true, otherwise, they are nothing more than neurons firing in the brain. In this practice, we do not believe we will die in x number of days. We hold this thought simply as an experiment to see how it impacts our moment-by-moment experience of life.

What this practice *can* do is to expose the hidden belief that we will *never* die, a belief that underlies all ego-identification. In exposing this (obvious) lie, we undermine the foundation of ego-identification. As we see through the lie, we immediately know the truth that our true identity is far greater than our ego-identification. This truth is then *experienced* rather than simply believed.

**2. Don't you believe in life after death? Doesn't life continue? If so, then why are we so concerned with dying?**

Yes, I believe in life after death, but I have no idea what that really means. This "life" that continues is unknown to my mind and to my senses. Everything my mind knows and my senses perceive is impermanent: It will all die.

The ego doesn't want to accept this because it undermines its "job security." As I accept the impermanency of all things—including my body and my mind (as I know it)—then I remove the barrier to experiencing life *as it truly is*, rather than as I believe it to be. This is the true experience of eternal life, which is lived every moment, regardless of the status of the physical body.

**3. Death will come soon enough and I will face it at that time; until then, why should I worry about it?**

Don't worry about it—that does no good whatsoever! Worry is the result of anticipation. This practice is not about anticipating our death; none of us knows when that will occur or what it will look like.

This practice is simply facing the fact that "someday I will die." In order to face that fact, I create a scenario to let me look at it directly, here and now, rather than pushing it off into some indefinite future. This practice is about becoming fully alive, which can happen only when I fully accept the mortality of this particular life-form called "me."

Listen to or download the audio meditation for this practice at *unitybooks.org/living*.

# 11. PRACTICE 9:
# LIVING IN THE HEART OF DESIRE

### What Is This Practice?

Upon reading the words "living in the heart of desire," many of us might think, *That sounds pretty easy; I've been doing it all my life!* None of us are strangers to feeling desire, and for some of us, certain desires have caused problems in our lives. However, this practice is much more than simply feeling how much or how often we desire something. To fully understand the nature and purpose of this practice, we need to unpack the term *desire* and its implications in our life.

Various spiritual traditions seem to have conflicting views on the role of desire in spiritual development. One school of thought is exemplified by these words of H. Emilie Cady, a noted New Thought writer: "What is desire? Desire in the heart is always God tapping at the door of your consciousness with His infinite supply ..."[35] She then goes on to assert that the very desire itself emanates from the "heart of God." This is a very provocative statement and has enormous implications, some of which I will address a bit later.

The converse of this perspective is portrayed within a body of teachings attributed to Siddhartha Gautama, who became known as "The Buddha." He has been quoted as saying, "Desire is the cause of all suffering." This statement is also very powerful—and very problematic. Many questions will arise: "How is one able to live without desire? Isn't desire innate in all living beings? Would we even be human if we had no desires? Isn't trying to overcome desire itself a desire?" All in all, this statement seems very difficult to accept.

Let's explore desire as "the cause of suffering." This statement relates to the second of the Four Noble Truths, which form the foundation of the Buddha's teaching. In this teaching, the word *desire* is translated from the Sanskrit word *tanha*, which literally means *thirst*. *Tanha* refers to desire in the form of *craving*, which is desire with *attachment* to the object of desire. Craving is desire that is fixated on a particular object as the sole source of its fulfillment. Desire with attachment might also be called *addiction*. It is desire with attachment, *not desire itself* that is problematic.

Desire is inherent in every form of life. Every animal and every human being experiences desire. Desire is necessary for the maintenance and continuity of physical life. Desire is not a bad thing, and we can't get rid of it—nor should we try.

The Buddha tells us suffering arises when we experience attachment to the object of our desire. Interestingly, the suffering is present whether we obtain the object of our desire or not. If we don't attain the object of our desire, then our suffering seems quite understandable; we all know the pain of an unfulfilled dream or an unrequited love. We are convinced our suffering is caused by the absence of the object of our desire. Yet the Buddha tells us suffering is inherent in attachment itself, regardless of the presence or absence of the desired object.

Even when I obtain the object of my desire, suffering will result if attachment is present. Nothing existing in time and space is permanent; everything in my life will someday be gone. The belief I can possess anything is an illusion. I don't even own my body or my mind—this, too, is impermanent. Attachment results in possessiveness and the fear of loss: I will suffer whether or not I obtain the desired object. If I am attached to anything or anyone I now "have," I will experience anxiety from the knowledge that someday this object or relationship can, and will, be gone; and someday *I* will be gone! Sooner or later I will lose everything to which I am attached. Any form of attachment will cause some form of suffering.

The genius of the Buddha's insight lies in recognizing not only is suffering independent of my desire's fulfillment, but it shows me it is also independent of the object of my desire. It is the attachment itself that causes suffering. It doesn't matter whether or not the object I desire is "good" or "bad." If attachment is present, so is suffering. It doesn't matter whether or not I "deserve" the object of my desire; if attachment is present, so is suffering. This insight undermines a basic supposition in our culture that "happiness lies in getting enough of what we really need."

A corollary to this teaching is that I can live a life of abundance as long as I am not trying to make any object the source of my happiness.* Material things can give us pleasure, and that is not inherently bad. The problem arises when we make these the primary value in our life.

Now let's return to the idea that "all desire emanates from God." This teaching also has enormous implications, and it, too, raises many questions. One obvious question is: "Are you telling me the desires of a drug addict, a rapist, or a suicide bomber are coming from God? That seems very difficult to believe!"

This teaching also seems to contain an obvious inconsistency evident at every sporting event, wherein you have fans at the stadium or field house who have quite opposite desires. "Does God want the Yankees or the Red Sox to win this ball game?" Answers to these questions are abundant and passionate, but quite contradictory!

In order to fully understand this teaching, we need to examine some specific words in Cady's statement. She writes, "Desire in the heart is always God tapping at the door of your consciousness with His infinite supply ..." The key to understand-

---

*I use the term "object" to also include a relationship, role, or identity.

ing this lies in the phrase "in the heart." Desire in the heart is not necessarily the same as desire "in the mind." All desire, at its origin, is life expressing itself, and all life is an expression of God. Desire "in the heart" refers to desire at its very origin, as it arises from the Source of life itself. When we can discern and skillfully express this divine impulse as it arises, we are living originally—in the fullest sense of those words.

Original desire is like pure water arising from an underground spring. That water meanders across a wide expanse of land before reaching the sea. Along the way, this once pure water can become quite polluted and filled with toxins that were not present at its source. Desire arising in the heart may be polluted by many layers of unconscious conditioning before it reaches the surface level of conscious recognition. This conditioning is biological, psychological, and sociological. We are deeply conditioned by our physiology, by our evolutionary history, by our personal history, and by the culture and the historical milieu in which we live.

Desire in the heart is simple and fundamental. Our most basic desire is to express pristine divine energy, which is our essential nature. Filtered through our human body and psyche, this appears as the desire to survive, to reproduce, to love and be loved, to learn and to express ourselves, and to have some influence over our personal destiny. These basic drives are then filtered through the complex conditioning of our personal and collective history. In contrast to the heart's desire, desire in the mind is complex and multifaceted; its forms are endlessly varied, and some of these desires may even conflict with one another. There are many pollutants that can infiltrate the mind-body system to color the final form of desire as it reaches conscious awareness.

Let's combine these two profound teachings to create the foundation for the practice of Living in the Heart of Desire. The foundation of this practice is to feel the deepest desires of the heart, with no attachment to the outcome. To experience the desire of the heart without attachment to outcome is to live in the *heart* of desire rather than in the mind of desire. To experience desire fully, without attachment to outcome, is to allow life to express itself through you unfettered and unfiltered by past conditioning. This is what it means to live originally.

Reading these words, one might legitimately ask, "How do I do this? I know what desire is, but how do I recognize 'desire in the heart,' and how do I experience it without attachment?" The first step in experiencing desire in the heart is to refrain from acting out every impulse you feel. Only when you experience the desire fully, without immediately acting upon it, can you begin to discern the heart's desire from conditioned desires. So we begin by learning to not immediately act upon our impulses.*

Be aware of the desire as it arises. How does it feel in your body? What sensations do you experience? What emotions are present? What thoughts emerge? What belief is fueling these thoughts? Let yourself experience the sensations, feelings, and thoughts that arise apart from any intention to act upon them.

If you find you are attached to an outcome, then just notice the experience of attachment. How does it feel? Are you aware of any suffering? How does that feel? Notice if you see any relationship between the attachment and the suffering. Let the experience of attachment be your teacher.

Don't believe any internal criticisms that arise. Don't judge a desire to be good or bad, and don't be concerned with whether it is attainable or not; just feel the desire fully, without taking any action. In this practice, there are no good desires or bad desires; there is just the experience of desire. And attachment is not good or bad; it is just there or it isn't.

---

*In the case of addictions that threaten life or well-being, it is very important to get outside help. This help can be in the form of a recovery group and/or psychological counseling.

Don't be concerned if you discover you have conflicting desires—this is quite normal. We have conflicting desires because we have many layers of conditioning that were deposited at different times in our personal and collective history. The human brain actually consists of three distinct sub-brains that have evolved over eons of time. These brains frequently disagree with one another. We may feel as if we have both a host of angels and a herd of beasts within us, both vying quite diligently for our attention!

Continuing to practice the Core Practices is essential. Self-awareness and self-acceptance are crucial skills in engaging the current practice. Our most recent practice was facing death; the current practice is about facing life—in a whole new way. In the practice of using death as our advisor, you became aware of attachments and embraced the inevitability of letting them all go. In the current practice, you become aware of your attachments and embrace the inevitability of letting them all go, and then you experience what internally arises as you no longer focus upon a specific object to make you happy. You then embrace life, not as a set of objects and relationships outside yourself, and not as a set of concepts and beliefs *about* life; you embrace life fully as it is experienced in this very moment. You then open to being fully alive in this moment, with deep awareness of body and mind and deep awareness of desire and feelings.

When you do this, you will have access to a source of wisdom that is obscured when we are attached to an outcome or identified with emotions. Then the process of deciding if, when, and how to act, becomes quite effortless. As you listen to desire in the heart, and experience it directly and deeply without impulsively acting it out, you will access the source wisdom, love, and power that knows exactly what to do and when to do it. From the Tao Te Ching: "The Tao of heaven … seems at ease, and yet it follows a plan."[36]

There is a primal intelligence behind every desire, but that intelligence can be obscured and distorted by unconscious psychological forces. Honor the intelligence behind every desire—no matter how crazy or sordid it may seem. Just keep asking, "What do I *really* desire?" and then notice what feelings emerge. Continue asking this question until you have reached the very heart of the desire. The poet Rainer Maria Rilke writes, "Let everything happen to you: beauty and terror. Just keep going. No feeling is final."[37]

To live in the heart of desire is to be fully open to the divine love and wisdom embedded deep within every desire. Author Gerald May sums it up quite well: "Authentic spiritual practice is nothing other than consecration in action. It is feeling your deepest desire, claiming it as freshly born hope, offering it to God, and consciously living it as fully as you can."[38]

**Why This Practice Is Transformative**

Desire is the core of human life. Every newborn infant is a bundle of needs.* The infant will experience pleasure when these needs are met, and pain when the needs are not. At a very young age, she begins to develop a strategy for getting these needs met. This strategy eventually coalesces into an ego structure, which she identifies as herself. Her identity becomes conflated with the strategy itself.

This strategy usually involves some type of bargain—some form of compromise: We give up something to get what we most want. Human needs are hierarchical; if necessary, we will forego some needs to get other needs met. For example, we may abandon the need for autonomy and self-determination in order to feel loved. We may abandon the need for love in order to survive and be safe. With every bargain, we gain something and

---

*Needs are universal human desires. In infancy, *desire* and *need* are synonymous. With conditioning, basic needs and desires will diverge.

we lose something. That which is lost seems less essential than which is gained; but the lost need does not disappear. The unfulfilled desire continues to reside painfully within us. It forever pushes toward fulfillment.

Identified with the strategy, we become attached to a specific outcome associated with the fulfillment of the need. In conducting his research on the digestion of dogs, Russian Nobel Prize physiologist Ivan Pavlov paired the ringing of a bell with the feeding of his experimental dog. He discovered that eventually, to the dog, the sound of the ringing bell was not just another sound; it meant food was on the way, and the dog would salivate in anticipation.[39] Similar to Pavlov's puppy, we learn to associate specific events or circumstances with the anticipated fulfillment of our basic needs.

For example, if I learned the only way to experience love and attention from my parents was to succeed at some endeavor and be publically recognized for my success, then I may become strongly attached to achievement and success, because I see this as a requirement for being loved. To me, success means love and attention; failure can mean rejection or shame. I seek achievement because I desire love. I may be driven to succeed even when it appears unnecessary, because the external goal is not the real prize, it is a counterfeit. Because it is a counterfeit, all the success in the world will not give me the love I desire any more than ringing a thousand bells will satisfy the dog's hunger.

We all experience the process of ego formation, which largely replaces the instinctual behaviors that are preprogrammed into most animals. For humans, culture replaces many instincts, which nature provides to other animals. Our conditioned behaviors may feel instinctive because they serve the same purpose as an animal's instincts: survival. My desire for success may feel every bit as strong as a child's desire for love from his parents.

Even if I consciously recognize this obsession with success is no longer serving me, trying to change it can be quite difficult because it feels like I would be giving up the desire to be loved. It will not seem like my adult self that is giving up the desire, but it will feel more like the needy child that developed the strategy in the first place. The loss can feel overwhelming.

As you feel desire fully, without attachment to a particular outcome, you will eventually experience the deeper need behind the conditioned desire. In my example, if I were to let myself feel the desire for success and recognition without taking action, and then bring attention to the thoughts, feelings, and sensations that arise, I will eventually see the desire for success is really just a camouflage for the desire to be loved.

If I allow myself to feel the desire for love directly and deeply, it will open my heart to the pain of the child who needed to be loved for being himself. Eventually, it will lead me to the very heart of love itself; it will lead me to my own essential nature, which is the origin of all love. Gerald May writes, "The secret of ... falling in love with life as it is meant to be, is to befriend our yearning instead of avoiding it, to live in our longing rather than trying to resolve it, to enter into the spaciousness of our emptiness instead of trying to fill it up."[40]

As we experience the primal desire directly, it leads us back to the very source of the desire, which is our own essential nature. Experiencing this source directly is the ultimate fulfillment of *every* desire. As we do this, we *will* hear God "tapping at the door of our heart." We can then experience desire as a form of guidance that directs our soul on its journey of awakening; this is living originally. Just as all animals have the instinct for survival, we have an instinct for spiritual awakening, but we must clear away the many layers of past conditioning to experience our own "GPS" (God's Perfect Solution).

This process is very powerful—and it is often quite painful. As we discover our attachments and defenses, and meet them directly rather than compulsively acting them out, we begin to experience the pain of the unmet needs and the unfelt feelings that have been hidden by our obsessive thinking and our compulsive behavior. Beneath this, we will experience the pain of our original self-abandonment, which is the abandonment of our heart's deepest desire to search for an external substitute.

We are like the Prodigal Son who left the house of his father and journeyed into the far country. Our work is to see how and why we left (and continue to leave) our original home and journeyed into the external world in search of the fulfillment of our heart's desire. As we see this clearly and then make the decision to return to the father's house, to our own essential nature, we will find the Father within waiting for us with open arms. As we make one step toward him, he makes 10,000 steps toward us.

It is very important to continue the Core Practices of self-awareness, self-acceptance, and forgiveness as you engage this current practice. Don't hesitate to seek peer support or professional help as needed. Pain is not the enemy; it can show us how we have unwittingly turned our back on that which is real. Pain can be our teacher; it can break down the walls that limit our awareness. Allow the wall around your heart to be broken open as your awareness expands in your journey back home to your essential nature.

## Forms of the Practice

The general form of each practice is to engage the practice in your everyday life. The current practice is largely internal; externally, simply live your life as you ordinarily would. Also, remember each special practice includes all the Core Practices.

As you live your everyday life, be aware of those things that seem to be attractors for any addictive or compulsive behavior. It may be particular foods or beverages, it may be certain behaviors such as gambling or shopping, and it may be associated with certain issues, such as love, power, security, money, or sexuality.

Be aware of the particular circumstances or events that seem to trigger unconscious or addictive behavior. For example, you may find whenever you feel stressed you always crave a glass of wine, or whenever you're lonely you desire sexual contact, or whenever you feel bored you have an urge to head for the casino. If you are able, be aware of the thoughts and emotions that immediately precede the urge to act out the desire.

Remember, our primary focus is not on behavioral change, but upon the transformation of consciousness. However, if you see your behavior is unethical or harmful to yourself or another, intervention may be necessary. In such a case, seek professional help and/or a Twelve-Step recovery program.

While engaging the practice, you may notice behavioral changes occurring with no conscious effort on your part. As long as these are not harmful or unethical, all you need to do is be aware of this and notice how you feel as you experience these behaviors. Don't be attached to any particular behavioral changes occurring or not occurring.

It's very important to remain nonjudgmental of yourself at all times. If judgments do arise, then just notice them, but don't believe them. See that it is simply an old pattern at work and refuse to believe this internal critic any longer. If the judgmental voice is harsh or punitive, then you may need to stand up to it with the resolve of a parent protecting her child, and say, "You have no right to treat me/her/him this way." Remain true to your authentic self.

We are not trying to get "somewhere" or "get over" anything. We are not trying to find answers to anything. This is simply an awareness practice.

As you engage this practice, be aware that you are aware. This way you can see you are much more than your desires; you are much more than your thoughts and your emotions. You are that which is aware.

Formal practice is setting aside a period of time to do nothing but some form of the practice itself. One type of formal practice is to do an inquiry into desire. The inquiry itself can take a number of different forms. One form of inquiry is to sit in a chair and bring the desire into your awareness. Then bring attention to your physical sensations. Notice how you experience this desire in your body; then notice what emotions, thoughts, or memories arise. Just be aware. Do this without analysis or interpretation. After the period of sitting, you can make notes in your journal, recording the experiences and insights that arose in the process.

If you are strongly attached to a particular object of desire, then you can inquire into that as well. (Remember that "object" can also mean a person, behavior, or experience.) In addition to feeling the desire as just described, feel what it would be like if you had obtained the object of your desire. Feel physical sensations, emotions; notice thoughts and beliefs. Do this practice for a designated period of time, and then feel what it would be like to *not* have the object of your desire; notice physical sensations, emotions, and thoughts. Record your experiences and insights.

You can also *dialogue* with the desire or with the object of desire. You can do this by journal-writing the dialogue or with the empty-chair process described in the previous chapter. You can also imagine the desire itself as an entity and have it speak, sing, paint, dance, or write poetry. (See Chapter 8 for a review of this process.)

You can also do the inquiry process with a partner. The partner should be someone with whom you feel safe and comfortable, and will be able to help you work the process. It should be someone who can be supportive and yet relatively unattached. (It is generally best not to work with a spouse, lover, or family member.)

Find a quiet, private space. Sit in a chair facing each other. Designate a period of time for the process: 10 to 20 minutes is suggested. Your partner will ask a series of repeating questions and you will respond spontaneously to each. It's very important your response be from the heart, unrehearsed and unedited. Stay aware of physical sensations and emotions as you do this. Be as aware of these experiences as you are of the words you speak.

It's very important the partner do nothing but ask the questions, with no verbal or nonverbal reaction or feedback. They are not counseling, coaching, or guiding you in any way; their job is to simply ask the questions and then be a supportive and neutral listening presence.

### Here are the questions for your partner to ask:

- "What do you want?" (You respond spontaneously, without thinking, analyzing, or editing. Just say whatever comes up.)
- Then your partner asks: "What would you feel if you had that?" (Respond again, without any editing.)
- The partner: "Then, what do you want?" After you respond, your partner says, "What would you feel if you had that?"

Continue this process of repeating the questions for the designated period of time. If either of you become confused, or the process comes to a halt, your partner can ask, "What are you feeling right now?" Also, "What do you want right now?"

At the end of the period, sit quietly with eyes closed for a few minutes, and then thank your partner. There should be no further discussion between the two of you regarding the content of the session. You may choose to swap roles and repeat the process, but it is not necessary.

## Perils on the Path

The far enemy of this practice is to neither wholeheartedly embrace your desires nor completely surrender your attachments. In other words, you are holding back the full passion of desire, yet never quite letting go of the object of desire. This is quite normal for the ego, which has learned to compromise its way through life.

The near enemy can take one of two primary forms. One form is to live fully in the experience of desire but remain unconsciously attached to a specific outcome. This is the experience of *addiction*. The other form of near enemy is the converse: to be nonattached to the outcome, yet never *fully* experience the passion of desire. This is the experience of resignation or apathy.

Let's explore the first form. It's likely the more common form because attachment to outcome is normative in our culture. For some of us, it may even be difficult to comprehend any difference between desire and attachment. But there is a difference: If we are attached, then suffering will appear when we do not get what we want. If we are nonattached, then we experience little or no suffering if our desired object does not materialize. Attachment and the resultant suffering usually exist on a continuum—it is rarely all or nothing. We usually have some degree of attachment to our desires; if we don't get what we want, then we will feel anything from mild disappointment to intense agony.

If you find you are attached to an outcome and seem unable to let go, just become aware of the feeling of attachment, as well as the thoughts and beliefs that accompany it. When you are attached to an outcome, you may feel fear of not getting what you want; you may feel anger if some obstacle seems to get in the way of your success; you may feel envy if someone else attains what you desire. Just notice all of this and then notice the suffering that quite naturally accompanies attachment. Awareness of suffering is the first step toward dissolving it.

See if you're willing to face the possibility of not getting what you desire. What does this feel like? Don't judge yourself for having the attachment—it is simply what's present at this time. If you're not willing to face the possibility of not getting what you desire, then feel that part of yourself that refuses to do this; feel the fear, and any other feelings present.

The second form of near enemy is to be nonattached to an outcome, but to never fully embrace the desire. If you feel nonattached to an outcome, then see if there is any suppression of desire. Sometimes we hedge our bets: "I won't let myself want this too much so I won't feel too disappointed if I don't get it." If you see this, then explore what it feels like to go "all out" with your desire; even if there is some attachment, let yourself have the full desire.

I might develop this as a strategy if, as a child, I was frequently disappointed by not getting what I wanted. I may have learned to "hold back" on fully feeling what I wanted as a way to assuage the pain of disappointment. If I continue to do this, then I will never allow myself to feel passionate about anything, and I never heal the grief that arose from my childhood disappointments.

In the previous chapter we heard about Zorba, the Greek, and his English friend, Basil. This was the strategy Basil had evidently adopted; he was afraid to completely embrace his desires, afraid to live his life fully. At one point Basil narrates, "I had fallen so low that, if I had had to choose between falling in love with a woman and reading a book about love, I should have chosen the book."[41] Before he met Zorba, he was living only the shell of a life. Zorba taught Basil to open to his desires and embrace his passion for life. However, Zorba may not be our best role model for this practice! He lived with passion, albeit not always in a skillful way—he needed some work on self-control and nonattachment. Yet it is quite possible to live our life with an open-hearted passion, and do so ethically and responsibly. That is the intention of this practice.

## FAQ

**1. I don't know how to experience desire without attachment; they seem to be the same thing to me.**

Don't try to be nonattached; just notice when attachment is present and then bring attention to your physical sensations, your emotions, and your thoughts. The ego will want to focus on the object of desire; just notice, but keep returning awareness to your own internal experience. Focus primarily on your own experiences rather than upon the object of desire. The purpose of the practice is to increase awareness, not to try for some idealized state of perfection.

**2. Why desire something if I know I can't have it? Isn't that just an exercise in frustration?**

It *can* be an exercise in frustration to the degree attachment is present. The object of this practice is to explore the experience of desire itself, without obsessing over the object of desire. Then the practice is *not* an exercise in frustration, but an opportunity for transformation.

Paradoxically, when you focus on the desire itself rather than upon external results, the object of your desire may be more likely to manifest—and often in some unexpected ways. Whatever it is, you may enjoy it even more, because you have released the expectation that this particular outcome is the source of your happiness. Our life circumstances can provide us much enjoyment when we stop expecting them to make us happy!

The world can bring us pleasure, but happiness comes only from within.

**3. What about the biblical commandments, "Thou shall not covet ..." (Ex. 20:17) and Jesus' teaching that "Lust in the heart is the same as committing adultery" (Mt. 5:28)? Doesn't this imply that "living in the heart of desire" can sometimes be sinful?**

If we are to discuss the issue of sin or morality, then we must consider the issue of volition, or free will. An act can be deemed "sinful" only if it is committed from free will. We assume animals do not sin because they do not have free will, as humans do. And yet, humans have many of the same basic desires as animals. The drives for survival and reproduction are not consciously chosen. They are inherent in human nature.

The key factor lies in how we respond to these desires that arise spontaneously. We may try to deny them, but that leads only to frustration—and perhaps neurosis. We may blindly act out these desires, which can lead to much suffering for ourselves and others.

A familiar compromise is to secretly harbor an obsession for the object of our desire, without overtly acting upon it. This is sometimes referred to as *coveting* or *lusting*. This may prevent the social difficulties that arise from acting out these desires, but it still creates much suffering for us.

This practice of "living in the heart of desire" is not about coveting or lusting after a particular outcome. It is about letting go of attachment to any particular outcome and then exploring the source of the desire itself. This can lead us to the realization that what we really want is not the object of our desire, but the very source of it: the ever-present origin.

**4. What's wrong with manifesting my desires through the power of the mind? Jesus said to pray, "Believing that you have received" (Mk. 11:24). Isn't *belief* the same as *attachment*?**

There is absolutely nothing wrong with manifesting the fulfillment of your desire through the power of the mind. However, if you think fulfilling the desires of the mind will make you happy, then you will become disillusioned. True happiness can be found only beyond the desires the mind endlessly presents to us. Repeating a previously mentioned quote of Jesus: "Seek first his kingdom ... and all these things shall be yours as well" (Mt. 6:33).

One definition of *attachment* is "the belief or feeling that obtaining the object of desire will bring happiness." This is not necessarily the same as believing I will receive (or have received) what I want. How I respond if I don't get what I want will indicate if attachment is present.

This discussion points out a key distinction between *translational* and *transformational* spirituality. The key question is, "What do I *really* want?" Transformational spirituality says, "I am willing to let go of what *I think I want* in order to experience *what I really want*—which is to experience my own true nature."

Listen to or download the audio meditation for this
practice at *unitybooks.org/living*.

# 12. PRACTICE 10:
# I AM THE AUTHOR OF MY LIFE

## What Is This Practice?

"You are the author of your life!" On stage was a well-known motivational speaker, and his message was, "Take charge of your life, and become a creator, rather than a victim." I was inspired by his words and have successfully applied many of his ideas in my life. I created the life I wanted ... or at least, thought I wanted.

Over time I began to see, deep down inside, I was actually not much happier than I had been before. I began to realize changing my life circumstances would not fulfill my heart's deepest desire. I discovered what I really wanted was not just different life conditions, but a different life. Although I did not have the language to articulate it, what I really wanted was *transformation* rather than translation.

Transformational spiritual practice does not focus on changing life circumstances, but focuses on changing the seeker herself. Transformational practice focuses not upon having what you want, but upon authentically being that which you truly are. What you truly are is infinitely more than anything the mind can conjure as necessary for happiness. Be what you truly are and you will always have what you truly want.

This practice is part of the process of actualizing your fullest potential. Another name for this process is *evolution*. The same life force and the same intelligence working to evolve life everywhere is working within you right now. The same power and intelligence that shaped the stars and galaxies is at work in your mind, in your heart, and in your life, right now. Transformative spiritual practice is a vital part of this evolutionary process.

The Jesuit priest and paleontologist Pierre Teilhard de Chardin developed a powerful visionary map of human possibility. His theory of evolution culminates in the development of all beings, led by humanity, into what he calls the Omega Point. The Omega Point is a hypothetical point in the future wherein humanity and the rest of creation become fully integrated into the conscious awareness of our oneness with God. This is the final culmination and the ultimate purpose of evolution. In Teilhard's view, evolution is not pushed by the past, but it is pulled by the future. It is not pushed from below, it is pulled from above, by Omega.

According to Teilhard, human consciousness is at the cutting edge of evolution on earth, and at the present time, humanity has reached the point where we must become responsible for our own evolution. Evolution is no longer happening to us, but through us. We are becoming evolution itself.

In the practice of I Am the Author of My Life, we take Teilhard's evolutionary model very personally. In this practice, I see myself as much more than simply the product of my personal history. I see myself as an integral part of a much larger story. I see my evolution is being pulled by the Omega Point, which individualizes as the divine potential within me. In this practice, I live my life as if I (as a personality) am a character in a story written by my divine potential—my own Omega-self. I then live my life with the premise that my future (Omega) self has written an autobiography in which I, the personality, am the lead character.

At the deepest level of your being, you are the author of your life; at the surface of your consciousness, you are but a character in a story authored by Omega. The divine potential within you is the author of this story, which is your life as you have experienced it. You, as you know yourself to be, are but a character in the story of the evolution of your personal self into Omega.

As you evolve spiritually, your identity shifts from the lead character to the author of this story. Ultimately, you are both the author and the character, simultaneously creating and experiencing your life as you know it. The awareness and the expression of Omega are the culmination, and the purpose, of the entire story, which is your soul's evolutionary journey.

Nothing in this story is predestined. Everything that unfolds in your life experience is the result of choices you have made. Until now, most of these choices were made unconsciously; based upon instinct or conditioning. Realizing you are the author of your life, you can make choices with an awareness of your true purpose. As you grow into awareness of Omega, you become the author of the story, rather than simply a character in it.

As you begin to live this story consciously, see that you are writing it as you are living it. Know you play a role in a much larger drama unfolding in every corner of our world. Your personal journey is an essential part of this greater story. As you enter into conscious authorship of your personal story, you begin to participate in the grand epic of life evolving on this planet.

Imagine your future self (Omega) has looked back in time and written its autobiography. Then live every minute of your life as if it were authored by your future self. The essence of this practice is to enter every experience as if you are both a character in the story and the author of it.

The practice is not concerned with what is or isn't true in a philosophical sense. It makes no difference whether or not you really believe any of this is true. You simply assume the truth of it as a hypothesis and live your life accordingly.

To fully engage this practice, you must suspend any belief that you are a victim of conditions or circumstances. You must suspend all blame or guilt and any belief in the reality of injustice. You need to be unattached to any judgments of what is good or bad, right or wrong. Use wisdom and discernment in the affairs of your life without being attached to any notion of absolute good or bad.*

This is an awareness practice. It doesn't focus on external changes, although your life circumstances may change as you engage the practice. If that happens, then see it as part of the unfolding story and notice your response to these changes. Remember to incorporate self-awareness and self-acceptance into all you do.

If some apparent misfortune occurs in your life, then do not feel guilt or self-recrimination. See that the experience of misfortune lies in the eyes of the character only, not in the eyes of the author. Yet it's still important to let yourself have your feelings about whatever has occurred; it's all part of the story.

The Zen master was weeping profusely upon the death of his son. A puzzled student approached him and said, "Master, you have told us that death is an illusion. Why are you weeping over the death of your son?" The master replied, "Yes, death is an illusion; and the death of my son is the greatest of all illusions!"

If some misfortune occurs to someone close to you, do not assume you, personally, are the cause of it; you are not. You are not the author of other people's stories, only your own. Don't be overly concerned with what other people's stories may mean; that is between them and their own true nature.

Allow your compassion to arise naturally, if it does. To each one of us, our suffering feels very real, and your ability to open your heart to others is a big part of your evolution. As we gain awareness of our own true nature, we see there really is only

---

*Discernment of good and bad can be useful within a certain context. However, it's important to see that these judgments are relative and contextual rather than absolute.

one Omega seeming to appear as different players in the grand drama of our evolution.

William Shakespeare wrote, "All the world's a stage, and all the men and women merely players."[42] In this practice, we develop the consciousness of a skilled actor, who is fully engrossed in his role, and yet deep inside knows he is more than the role: He has an identity, which will endure long after the play is over. We know we are also the playwright, having written the play for a specific purpose, a purpose to be discovered only by consciously entering into the role as impeccably as possible.

## Why This Practice Is Transformative

Transformational spiritual practice allows us to discover a reality that lies deeper than the rational mind and the senses. The practice challenges the ego's belief that it alone is capable of understanding and controlling our life. The ego (personal self) normally functions as "central command" for what is real, just, and correct in our life and our world. In this practice, though, the ego is relegated to a less exalted position. It is no longer the playwright, or even the director of our life drama; it is simply an actor. It plays a lead role, but it is only an actor in the evolutionary drama.

The ego has a counterpart: the Omega-self, which is an infinitely older and wiser version of itself. It authors the story. The only separation between these two versions of self is our limited awareness. Evolution is simply awareness unfolding through time, bringing you ever closer to the recognition that, at the deepest level, you are Omega.

As you engage this practice over time, your primary identity will gradually shift from lead character to author. You won't lose your personal identity as an actor, but you gain a much larger identity as the actor/author. Omega gradually becomes a very clear and present reality in your life. From this perspective, you see that nothing is predetermined, and nothing is impossible, because *you* are writing the story.

In truth, Omega and personal self are not separate; they are different versions of the same reality. They appear to be different when we are identified with the ego, embedded within time and space. The personal self (ego) is but a reflection of Omega, existing beyond time and space. They may appear to be separate, but as we evolve, we will see these two selves are really one.

To discover my true identity in Omega, I must see the many ways I am attached to the exclusive identity of personal self. I am identified with the ego when I experience fear or hatred and whenever I am resisting life as it is. When identified with the personal self, I will experience suffering.

Pleasure and pain are inevitable parts of being alive, but suffering is not inevitable. Pain and suffering are not the same thing. Suffering is the mental anguish that results from resisting life as it unfolds. Suffering is not a form of punishment; it is simply a natural consequence of attempting to live in opposition to reality.

To the degree I ascribe an independent reality to the ego self, I will experience suffering. As discussed in earlier chapters, the ego, or personal identity, is formed from an attempt to control my life experience rather than fully live it. Yet I can use my experience of suffering to see how I have separated from my true self (Omega). As soon as I see how I am identified with the personal self, I immediately begin to disidentify from it. By seeing attachment and resistance clearly, without judgment, I automatically begin to dissolve ego-identification.

This practice will highlight my awareness of attachment and resistance to life as it is. As I assume authorship of my life story, I begin to see more clearly the times I do not take responsibility for my life experience. I see when I believe I am a victim of others, or of life itself; and I see the ways I try to blame others for my suffering. To see all this without judgment or self-recrimination is very liberating. Nonjudgmental awareness is the solvent that dissolves attachment and suffering. As resistance and attachment are dissolved, the apparent separation between personal and Omega-self disappears.

Life can bring us experiences that make it seem as if we've been victimized by someone or something. To the extent we ascribe an absolute reality to this, we will suffer. To the extent we can see this as a necessary part of the story of evolution toward Omega, we will be free from that suffering.

Becoming part of the larger story doesn't mean you must negate your feelings or repress your pain; that does not lead to transformation. Feel each response to your life experiences deeply and completely. Act as if everything you do matters to the utmost. Give life all you've got, and yet, always remember it is just a story! Live your life consciously and impeccably; and then let it all go. Let the story unfold as it does. See *every* experience as a necessary step in your journey toward Omega.

Carlos Castaneda's teacher, Don Juan, attempted to teach him a similar practice, which he referred to as *controlled folly*. Don Juan speaks of one who is living originally as a "man of knowledge." He describes this person's actions: "... a man of knowledge chooses any act, and acts it out as if it matters to him. His controlled folly makes him say that what he does matters and makes him act as if it did, and yet he knows that it doesn't; so when he fulfills his acts he retreats in peace ..."[43]

An important part of the practice is to notice when you are unable to engage the practice. This might occur in a time of great pain or difficulty. For example, you may experience being the victim of an apparent injustice. This can be very painful and it may be difficult to experience this as simply a story; it may appear very real. Remain true to yourself, feel what you feel, and do what you do. As soon as you are able, return to the practice, without any judgment or self-recrimination. See that getting lost in the story is also part of the evolutionary journey.

Remember, a primary purpose of these practices is to see where we get stuck, to see when and how we are identified with the ego. The intention of this practice is not to do it "right," but to *just do it,* and to see when and why we are unable to do it. Don't try to change anything; just be aware. This is how we become free.

Also, notice when you *do* feel a sense of freedom or empowerment resulting from the practice. As you gradually shift identity from ego to Omega-self, you may experience a sense of peace, freedom, and power unlike anything accessible to the personal self. You can experience Omega as a timeless reality that resides at the deepest core of your being. Omega is the ever-present origin of consciousness itself.

It is very possible to experience this reality and to live fully impassioned and empowered in the world. This is the epitome of the ancient wisdom that encourages us to be fully in the world, but not of it. You then become evolution in action. This is what it means to live originally.

### Forms of the Practice

The general form of this practice is to live your everyday life through the lens of the lead character in a drama written by your own higher self: Omega. Your work is to live the role impeccably, and in so doing, you will begin to understand the deeper meaning of the story. As in a Greek drama, the actor is not depicting just a personal drama, but is living out a greater story that addresses the fundamental questions of what it means to be human.

The author of the drama is a much older and wiser part of yourself that can become a mentor and guide to the personal self, if you so choose. As you deepen your relationship with Omega, you begin to participate in writing the drama yourself. And you will see the drama is not finished; it is a work in progress. You also begin to see your personal drama is not separated from a much greater story that involves every living being on this planet.

To engage this practice with integrity, you need to see the times when you are not living your part as actor/author. It is very important to do this honestly and without self-judgment. A big part of doing the practice is to see when we are not doing the practice! This is where the learning takes place. Transformation always occurs at the outer edges of our capabilities.

There may be times when the story may call for us to be victimized in some way. Perhaps some property is stolen or you are injured by another person. At that time, you are in the role of a victim, but there is a huge difference between experiencing the role of victim and *being* a victim. This is not easy, and we may get lost at times; but that is the nature of spiritual practice. The intention isn't to "never get lost," but rather to see when that happens and then consciously return to the practice. This is how transformation occurs.

There are many ways to do the formal practice. One way is to simply sit quietly and focus attention on your heart center and rest your identity in Omega. Watch thoughts come and go, and return to the awareness of Omega at your center. Don't look for anything in particular; just be present to whatever arises into awareness. After sitting for 20 minutes, spend some time with your journal; record whatever thoughts or feelings arise from your heart, without editing or analyzing. Do this over a period of several days, and periodically review what you've written.

At the end of each day, you may record in your journal those times when you've felt centered and connected with a deeper reality, as well as those times when you've had difficulty engaging the practice. Record your feelings and the circumstances surrounding these experiences. You may discover some patterns!

You may periodically engage in a dialogue with Omega. You can do this verbally or in writing. If done verbally, you can record it electronically. Notice what you feel as you engage in the dialogue. After recording the dialogue, pause and read what was written, or listen to the recording. Notice what you experience as you review it. It is helpful to keep records of your dialogue over a period of time. You may be quite amazed at what can unfold when you create the time and space for it!

An interesting process is to write a brief autobiography of your life as if you are Omega, the author. Refer to the main character, your personal self, in the third person, by name. Write passionately and yet as objectively as possible. Look for the underlying theme or message you see in this story. How does the lead character develop? What does the rest of the story look like? How does it end?

## Perils on the Path

A common far enemy of this practice is to get lost in unconscious egoic patterns and forget about the practice. We may encounter a life situation that seems very serious, and very "real," and the practice can seem irrelevant to us. When anxious or stressed, we tend to revert to old patterns of thinking, feeling, and behavior. This is especially true when circumstances seem to justify our story. For example, if we are the victim of a crime or an accident, then it's easy to revert to an old pattern of blame or self-pity; and it's easy to find others who will support our story!

The great irony is that spiritual practice can be of greatest benefit to us when it is the most difficult to engage, and when we can find every reason on earth not to do it! When the deeply entrenched egoic patterns are activated, it's a great opportunity to become more conscious and less identified with these patterns. This is how we become free of them.

The near enemy of transformative spiritual practice is to consciously believe we're engaging the practice but unconsciously use it to fortify the ego-identification. An example is to use this practice to avoid experiencing some feelings or avoid being fully authentic. We might shrug off some painful feelings and say, "It's only a story," as a way to not feel these feelings and to not be fully present to the experience.

Another near enemy is to blame yourself if you experience an apparent misfortune. We might think, "What is wrong with me for having created this experience?" Or on the other hand, we might use the practice as a way to escape personal responsibility. An example might be to harm another person and then rationalize it by saying, "Their higher self must have authored that experience."

To engage this practice, it is very important we let go all blame, guilt, and self-pity. Yet we are still accountable for our actions; in none of our practices do we ever condone unethical or irresponsible behavior.

The Buddha gave a teaching titled "The Simile of a Snake" wherein he likens spiritual teachings to that of a snake: It must be grasped very skillfully, else it can "bite us" and cause much suffering.[44] These practices are very powerful transformative tools but can be problematic if used without clear understanding. It is very important to engage all our practices skillfully, ethically, and wisely.

Transformational spiritual practice is not a creed or a philosophy of life; we are not trying to feel a certain way, reach a goal, or solve a problem. Our primary intention is to simply engage the chosen practice without attachment to a specific outcome. As we do this, we shift our identity from the ego to the authentic self. As our identity shifts, so does our experience of reality. Transformation propels us into the experience of living authentically and originally in every facet of our life.

## FAQ

**1. Are you implying predestination? Are you saying our life story is already "written"?**

Remember, this is a hypothesis we are assuming for the sake of spiritual practice; it is not a statement of what is true or untrue in any metaphysical sense. I will respond according to the perspective we assume as we employ this practice.

The only thing predestined is we will someday realize our oneness with Omega (God). This is "predestined" only because it is already true, even though we may not be aware of it. How the process of realization unfolds within time and space is not predestined. It is largely up to us.

Yet we each have habituated patterns of thinking, feeling, and relating. We each carry deeply held beliefs, many of which are unconscious. These patterns create a strong propensity for certain life experiences to unfold in a predictable way.

When it rains, there is no predestined path for a particular raindrop to follow, yet it is fairly easy to predict the general direction rainwater will flow simply by studying the terrain upon which it lands. Rainwater has no power of choice, so gravity will direct its course.

To the extent we lack self-awareness, we are like the rainwater following the path of least resistance. In this sense, our path is quite predictable, and may appear predetermined. To the extent we gain self-awareness, we acquire the power of choice. As we become more aware, we are able to choose our own direction. Yet even though we have the power of choice, some of the "grooves" in consciousness created from the past may be very deep and very compelling. At times it may *feel* as if we have no choice, but we always do.

In this practice, we assume the ultimate power of choice arises not from the personal self but from our true self, which we are calling "Omega." Our personal self is seen to be like the rainwater falling into "old grooves" in the mind. Personal self may feel as if it has no choice when attempting to act independently, but it is capable of gaining the true freedom of choice as it recognizes its oneness with Omega. The purpose of this practice is to help the personal self experience this realization.

**2. I have an important decision to make; should I assume it's already been made by my Omega-self? How do I (personally) know what to choose?**

The intention of the practice is not to turn your life over to some hypothetical self. You, as personal self, are the operative agent in your life. But as you align the personal self with Omega, personal self has access to wisdom that is not available when it tries to act independent of the higher self. Personal self does not abdicate responsibility for the decision, but its choice is informed by wisdom far beyond its own level of understanding.

**3. Are you saying the suffering of millions of people on earth has been "authored" by their Omega-self? That sounds rather diabolical!**

No, I am not saying that. This practice does not attempt to answer the question of human suffering. It does not attempt to answer any specific question at all. It is simply a practice designed to enrich the life of the practitioner by discovering his or her own true nature.

The practice includes the hypothetical assumption that our personal self is not the totality of who we are, and there is a self (Omega), which is ontologically more real than the personal self. This Omega-self has authored our life, and we (personal self) have the opportunity to participate in this authorship as we discover and identify more closely with our true nature, Omega.

Listen to or download the audio meditation for this practice at *unitybooks.org/living*.

# EPILOGUE

At the close of my weekly meditation group, we say a prayer that ends with the words, "May my practice be of benefit to all beings." The purpose of this prayer is to affirm our intention that our spiritual practice be not for ourselves alone but for the benefit of all persons and all living beings everywhere.

Ultimately, this may be true regardless of our acknowledged intention because we cannot awaken spiritually in isolation from other beings. This is because the very heart of spiritual awakening is recognizing we are not separate from other beings. The deeper I go into myself, the more I find all of humanity residing there. The deeper into my humanness I delve, the more I experience my connection with every being in this universe.

Perhaps the greatest paradox of the spiritual journey is the mystery of our aloneness and our connectedness. On one hand, I am always alone, even if I am sitting in the middle of all my friends and family members. No matter how intimate I may be with another, my life can only be experienced by me alone. No one else can have my experience of life in this moment.

Yet I discover as I become more intimate with my own experience of life in each moment, I enter more deeply into the heart of life itself. To become intimate with oneself is to transcend the personal self; to transcend this self is to become intimate with all life. "May these spiritual practices be of benefit to all beings everywhere."

# ENDNOTES

1  *The Wisdom Way of Knowing: Reclaiming an Ancient Tradition to Awaken the Heart* (San Francisco: Wiley), 86-87.

2  This term was coined by Jean Gebser in his book *The Ever-Present Origin* (1949).

3  I first encountered this term in Ken Wilber's book *One Taste* (Shambhala, 1999).

4  Matthew 13:45-46.

5  The term *Right Intention* is borrowed from the Buddhist teaching of the Eight-Fold Path. I am using this term in a similar way, but I am not confining my discussion to Buddhism or any other specific spiritual or religious system.

6  The remaining text in this chapter has been adapted from the 2000 Unity pamphlet *Transformation* by Robert Brumet. Published by Unity, 1998.

7  Ralph Waldo Emerson, "Self-Reliance," *Essays by Ralph Waldo Emerson* (New York: Harper and Row, 1926),  38.

8  Ibid., 32.

9  Rachel Naomi Remen, *Kitchen Table Wisdom: Stories That Heal* (New York: Berkley, 1996), 139-140.

10  *Krishnamurti in India, 1970-71: Authentic Reports of Talks* (1971), Krishnamurti Foundation India. OCLC 639846008. Retrieved from http://wikiquote.org/wiki/Jiddu_Krishnamurti#Freedom_From_the_Self_.281955.29, September 14, 2012.

11  Charles Fillmore, *Dynamics for Living* (Unity Village, MO: Unity Books, 1967), 52.

12  Fillmore refers to this as *"the indwelling Father."*

13 Rachel Naomi Remen. *Ibid.* 29-30.

14 *No Boundary: Eastern and Western Approaches to Personal Growth* (Boston: Shambhala, 1979), 152.

15 This story was shared at a retreat at the Insight Meditation Society in Barre, MA, in May 2009.

16 William Shakespeare, *The Merchant of Venice*, Act 4, Scene 1, 180–187.

17 Adapted from Jack Kornfield, and Christina Feldman, *Soul Food: Stories to Nourish the Spirit and the Heart.* (New York: Harper San Francisco, 1996), 331-32. I have also heard Jack Kornfield tell this story at an Insight Meditation retreat.

18 Republic 354c.

19 Lao Tsu, *Tao Te Ching* (New York: Random House, 1972). Translated by Gia-Fu Feng and Jane English, No. 22.

20 *Thus Spoke Zarathustra: A Book for All and None,* Walter Kaufmann (Translator) (New York: Random House, 1995), 17. (*Thus Spake Zarathustra.* Zarathustra's Prologue, Part 5; 1891).

21 As quoted in Joel and Michelle Levey, *Living in Balance* (Berkeley, CA: Conari Press, 1998), 20.

22 From *Tao Te Ching* by Lao Tsu, translated by Gia-fu Feng and Jane English, translation copyright © 1972 by Gia-fu Feng and Jane English, copyright renewed 2000 by Carol Wilson and Jane English. Used by permission of Alfred A. Knopf, a division of Random House, Inc. Any third party use of this material, outside of this publication, is prohibited. Interested parties must apply directly to Random House, Inc., for permission.

23 Karlfried Graf Durckheim quoted in Greg Levoy, *Callings: Finding and Following an Authentic Life* (New York Crown Publishers, 1997), 258.

24 http://www.famousquotesabout.com/by/Gregory-Col bert, July 5, 2012 (Accessed August 25, 2012).

25 *Four Quartets* (New York: Harcourt, Brace and Company). Excerpt from "Burnt Norton" Part II in *Four Quartets* by T. S. Eliot, copyright 1936 by Harcourt, Inc., and renewed 1964 by T.S. Eliot, reprinted by permission of Houghton Mifflin Harcourt Publishing Company. All rights reserved.

26 David Shainberg. As quoted in John Biggs and David Peat, *Seven Life Lessons of Chaos: Spiritual Wisdom From the Science of Change* (New York: Harper Collins, 1999), 29.

27 John Biggs and David Peat, *Seven Life Lessons of Chaos: Spiritual Wisdom From the Science of Change* (New York: Harper Collins, 1999), 64-65.

28 Carlos Castaneda, *Journey to Ixtlan: The Lessons of Don Juan* (New York: Simon and Schuster, 1972), 33.

29 Ibid., 34.

30 Ibid.

31 http://www.csun.edu/science/health/docs/tv&health.html (Accessed August 25, 2012).

32 *Setting Your Heart on Fire: Seven Invitations to Liberate Your Life* (New York: Random House, 2003), 114.

33 http://en.wikipedia.org/wiki/Jesus_Christ_Superstar. Lyrics by Tim Rice, 1971 (Accessed December 5, 2012).

34 Kathleen Dowling Singh, *The Grace in Dying* (New York: Harper Collins, 2000).

[35] H. Emilie Cady, *Lessons in Truth* (Unity Village, MO: Unity School of Christianity, 1941), 65.

[36] Tao Te Ching, ibid.

[37] *Rilke's Book of Hours: Love Poems to God,* translated by Anita Barrows and Joanna Macy. (Berkley Publishing Group, 1996), 88.

[38] Gerald May, *The Awakened Heart: Opening Yourself to the Love You Need* (New York: Harper Collins, 1991), 111.

[39] Ivan Pavlov (1849–1936) was a famous Russian physiologist. He is most well-known for his experiment in which dogs were fed immediately after the ringing of a bell. The food caused the dogs to salivate at first, but after repeated presentations of bell/food, *the bell itself* caused the dogs to salivate.

[40] Ibid., 104.

[41] Nikos Kazantzakis, *Zorba the Greek* (New York: Simon and Schuster, 1952), 101.

[42] William Shakespeare, *As You Like It*, Act II, Scene VII.

[43] Carlos Castaneda, *A Separate Reality: Further Conversations With Don Juan* (New York: Simon and Schuster, 1971), 85.

[44] Alagaddupama Sutta, *The Middle Length Discourses of the Buddha: A New Translation of the Majjhima Nikaya,* (Boston: Wisdom Publications, 1995), 227.

# ABOUT THE AUTHOR

**Robert Brumet** is the author of *Birthing a Greater Reality, Finding Yourself in Transition,* and *The Quest for Wholeness.* A frequent contributor to *Unity Magazine®,* he is also an ordained Unity minister and teaches courses in pastoral counseling, meditation, and spiritual development at Unity Institute® and Seminary in Unity Village, Missouri.

B0113